food network magazine

THE
BIG, FUN
KIDS
COOKBOOK

kids
HEARST
HOME

Food Network Magazine

Editor in Chief Maile Carpenter
Creative Director Deirdre Koribanick
Executive Editor Liz Sgroi
Managing Editor Robb Riedel
Photo Director Alice Albert

FEATURES
Deputy Editor Jessica Dodell-Feder
Food Editor Ariana Phillips Tessier
Special Projects Editor Pamela Mitchell
Associate Food Editor Kate Trombly O'Brien
Assistant Editor Cory Fernandez

ART AND PHOTOGRAPHY
Art Director Ian Doherty
Associate Art Director Amy Kaffka
Associate Photo Editor Amy McNulty
Digital Imaging Specialist Ruth Vázquez

COPY
Copy Chief Chris Jagger
Research Chief Katherine Wessling
Copy Editor David Cobb Craig

FOOD NETWORK KITCHEN
Executive Chef, Vice President, Culinary Production
Robert Bleifer
Vice President, Culinary Jill Novatt
Test Kitchen Director Stephen Jackson
Recipe Developers Melissa Gaman, Young Sun Huh,
Alexis Pisciotta, Amy Stevenson
Recipe Developer/Nutritionist Leah Brickley
Recipe Tester Amanda Neal

HEARST HOME KIDS
Vice President & Publisher Jacqueline Deval
Editor Nicole Fisher

HEARST MAGAZINE MEDIA, INC.
President Troy Young
Chief Content Officer Kate Lewis
Executive Vice President,
Chief Financial Officer & Treasurer Debi Chirichella
Secretary Catherine A. Bostron

Publishing Consultants Gilbert C. Maurer, Mark F. Miller

HEARST
President & Chief Executive Officer Steven R. Swartz
Chairman William R. Hearst III
Executive Vice Chairman Frank A. Bennack, Jr.

Library of Congress Cataloging-in-Publication Data is available.

10 9 8 7 6 5 4

Published by Hearst Home Kids, an imprint of Hearst Books/
Hearst Magazine Media, Inc.
300 West 57th Street
New York, NY 10019

Food Network Magazine and the Food Network Magazine logo are registered trademarks of Television Food Network, G.P. Hearst Home Kids, the Hearst Home Kids logo, and Hearst Books are registered trademarks of Hearst Magazine Media, Inc.

Printed in China.

ISBN 978-1-950785-04-9

To all the
junior chefs:
Keep cooking!

CONTENTS

You've probably seen kids do some pretty amazing things on Food Network. They've whipped up mirror glazes on *Kids Baking Championship,* grilled lobsters on *Kids BBQ Championship* and butchered snakes on *Chopped Junior.* Don't worry—we don't expect you to do any of that! This cookbook is full of recipes that any kid can make, even if the only thing you've ever done in the kitchen is eat.

Ready to get cooking? First you have to decide what to make! We photographed every recipe in this book, and we put all the photos in the index on page 8 so you can shop for your next project. Some recipes are as simple as spreading toppings on toast, while others require a little more time—and help from an adult. (You probably shouldn't break out a propane tank and blow-torch a cake just yet! Though it's pretty fun to watch; see pages 162 and 174.)

We tested the recipes in this book like crazy to make sure they'd come out OK for you, but if you mess up from time to time, no problem: That's how you learn. Here's a little secret from the test kitchen: Everybody makes mistakes. And we mean *everybody.* Valerie Bertinelli (the beloved judge from *Kids Baking Championship*) once whisked a béchamel sauce so hard she sent it flying all over her kitchen and kept finding specks of it for weeks after! Guy Fieri once put too much oil in the pot when he was frying a turkey and basically created a fireball in his yard. And a chef competing on *Chopped* once used salt instead of sugar in the dessert round. He lost the competition, but he still had a reason to be proud: He made it to the final round!

The good news is, you won't be cooking in front of a camera or racing to beat a countdown clock when you're making these recipes. Take your time, ask for help when you need it, and most of all, have fun! Oh, and don't forget to show us what you made: Post it with #FNMkids.

Maile Carpenter
Editor in Chief

Liz Sgroi
Executive Editor

BREAKFAST

Raisin-Walnut
Grilled Cheese
38

Pizza
Grilled
Cheese
39

French Grilled Cheese
38

Hoagie
Grilled Cheese
39

Ham-and-Cheese
Wafflewiches with
Kale Chips
41

Ham and Cheese
Noodle Salad
53

Fresh Tomato Soup
with Grilled Ham
and Cheese
46

Design-Your-Own
Chicken Salad
43

LUNCH

Cuban Beef
Pockets
50

Curried
Chicken
Pockets
51

Open-Face
English Muffin
Sandwiches
44

Taco Salad
Cups
49

RECIPE INDEX

SNACKS

DINNER

RECIPE INDEX

DESSERT

FAKE-OUT CAKES

Hey, bacon and egg fans, see page 27!

14

Breakfast

Did You Know?

Waffles inspired Nike's first running shoe:
Company cofounder Bill Bowerman was having breakfast
when he realized that the grooves in his waffle iron
would make a great mold for the sole of a sneaker!

Classic Waffles

ACTIVE: 20 min   TOTAL: 20 min   MAKES: 10 to 12

5   tablespoons vegetable shortening

4   tablespoons unsalted butter, plus more for topping

2   cups all-purpose flour

4   teaspoons baking powder

2   tablespoons sugar

1   teaspoon salt

2   large eggs

1½ cups milk

Cooking spray

Pure maple syrup, for topping

1 Microwave the shortening and butter in separate small microwave-safe bowls until melted.

2 Combine the flour, baking powder, sugar and salt in a large bowl and whisk to combine. Add the eggs, milk, melted shortening and melted butter and whisk until just combined (it's OK if there are some lumps).

3 Preheat a waffle iron and coat with cooking spray. Slowly pour ⅓ to ½ cup batter into the hot waffle iron with a ladle or measuring cup (the batter should be about 1 inch from the edge of the iron). Close the waffle iron and cook until the waffles are crisp. Carefully remove the waffles with a rubber spatula or tongs and place them on a wire rack to cool. Repeat with the remaining batter to make more waffles. Serve the waffles with butter and maple syrup.

Tip

Keep your leftover waffles to eat as toaster waffles: Just cool them on a wire rack, freeze in resealable plastic bags and pop into a toaster for a quick breakfast!

Pancakes with Chocolate-Banana Crunch

ACTIVE: 25 min   TOTAL: 25 min   MAKES: 6 to 8

FOR THE PANCAKES

4   tablespoons unsalted butter

1½ cups all-purpose flour

3   tablespoons sugar

1½ teaspoons baking powder

½   teaspoon salt

¼   teaspoon baking soda

1   cup plus 2 tablespoons milk

1   large egg

Cooking spray

FOR THE TOPPINGS

4   ounces semisweet chocolate

3   tablespoons heavy cream

2   tablespoons honey

1   banana, sliced

Granola, for topping

1   Make the pancakes: Microwave the butter in a small microwave-safe bowl until melted.

2   Combine the flour, sugar, baking powder, salt and baking soda in a medium bowl and whisk to combine. Combine the milk, melted butter and egg in a separate medium bowl and whisk to combine. Add the milk mixture to the flour mixture and whisk until just combined (it's OK if there are some lumps).

3   Heat a large nonstick skillet or griddle over medium-low heat and coat with cooking spray. Pour in ¼ cup of the batter with a ladle or measuring cup for each pancake and cook until bubbly on top and golden on the bottom, about 4 minutes. Flip with a spatula and cook until golden on the other side, about 2 more minutes. Remove the pancakes and place on a plate.

4   Make the toppings: Carefully chop the chocolate with a chef's knife. Combine the chopped chocolate, heavy cream and honey in a small microwave-safe bowl. Microwave 30 seconds, then stir with a spoon. Continue to microwave, stirring every 30 seconds, until the sauce is smooth. Top the pancakes with the banana slices, chocolate sauce and granola.

Tip
You'll know your pancakes are ready to flip when you see bubbles on the batter.

French Toast Pigs in a Blanket

ACTIVE: 20 min   TOTAL: 40 min   MAKES: 12

12 breakfast sausage links
6   large eggs
¾   cup milk
¼   cup granulated sugar
¼   teaspoon
     ground cinnamon
Pinch of ground nutmeg
Pinch of salt
12 slices potato bread or
     country white bread
4   tablespoons unsalted
     butter
Confectioners' sugar,
     for topping
Pure maple syrup,
     for dipping

1 Preheat the oven to 375°. Line a baking sheet with parchment paper. Put the sausages on the baking sheet and bake until lightly browned and cooked through, about 10 minutes. Remove the pan from the oven with oven mitts and let cool slightly.

2 Meanwhile, combine the eggs, milk, granulated sugar, cinnamon, nutmeg and salt in a large bowl and whisk to combine. Cut each slice of bread into a 2-by-4-inch rectangle with a chef's knife, cutting off the crusts, then press the bread gently with your fingertips to flatten slightly. Starting at a short end, roll each piece of bread around a sausage link, pressing firmly with your fingers to seal the seam. Add the bread-wrapped sausages to the bowl with the egg mixture and let soak for 5 minutes.

3 Melt 2 tablespoons butter in a large nonstick skillet over medium heat. Remove 6 of the bread-wrapped sausages from the egg mixture, letting the excess egg drip back into the bowl, then add to the skillet. Cook, turning occasionally with a spatula, until golden brown, about 5 minutes.

4 Carefully remove the pigs in a blanket to paper towels using the spatula. Bunch up a paper towel and hold it with tongs to wipe out the skillet. Add the remaining 2 tablespoons butter to the skillet and repeat with the other 6 bread-wrapped sausages.

5 Sprinkle the confectioners' sugar over the wrapped pigs in a blanket. Serve with maple syrup for dipping.

Tip

To keep these warm until you're ready to eat, place them on a wire rack set on a baking sheet in a 250° oven. You can do the same with pancakes and waffles.

Did You Know?

French toast isn't actually French. The dish can be traced back to the Roman Empire—long before France was even a country! Why do we call it French? Some say that an innkeeper named Joseph French coined the term, but no one knows for sure.

Stuffed French Toast

Cream Cheese + Blackberry Jam + Pistachios

Ricotta + Apricot Jam

Chocolate-Hazelnut Spread + Bananas

Marshmallow Cream + Raspberry Jam

❶ Pick a Filling

Place ½ cup of one of the following ingredients in a medium bowl.

Softened cream cheese   **Mashed banana**   **Ricotta cheese**   **Marshmallow cream**

❷ Add Mix-Ins

Stir in ¼ cup total of the following ingredients (choose 1 or 2).

Jam, jelly or marmalade   **Peanut butter or other nut butter**   **Chocolate-hazelnut spread**   **Speculoos (cookie butter)**

Chocolate chips   **Peanut butter chips**   **Chopped nuts**   **Raisins**   **Chopped berries**

❸ Stuff the Bread

Carefully cut four 1½-inch-thick slices from a loaf of challah bread with a serrated knife. With the bread slices flat on a cutting board, carefully cut a 2- to 3-inch-wide slit into the bottom edge of each bread slice with a paring knife to create a deep pocket Ⓐ. Put the filling in a resealable plastic bag and snip a corner. Pipe some filling into each pocket Ⓑ.

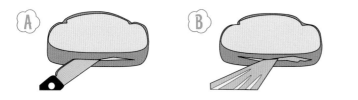

❹ Make the Custard

Combine 2 eggs, 1 cup half-and-half, 1 tablespoon granulated sugar, 1 teaspoon vanilla, ½ teaspoon ground cinnamon, ¼ teaspoon ground nutmeg and a pinch of salt in a shallow bowl and whisk until combined.

❺ Cook the French Toast

Preheat the oven to 250°. Dip a stuffed bread slice in the custard and soak 20 seconds per side; let the excess drip off and place on a plate. Repeat with the remaining bread slices. Heat a large nonstick skillet over medium heat. Melt 1 tablespoon butter in the skillet, then add 2 stuffed bread slices and cook until browned, 4 to 5 minutes per side. Place on a baking sheet and keep warm in the oven. Bunch up a paper towel and hold it with tongs to wipe out the skillet. Repeat with more butter and the other 2 stuffed bread slices. Serve with maple syrup.

S'mores Muffins

ACTIVE: 25 min TOTAL: 1 hr (plus cooling) MAKES: 12

1   cup milk chocolate chips
1   cup all-purpose flour
1   stick unsalted butter,
     cut into pieces
1½   cups graham cracker
     crumbs (from about
     15 whole crackers)
2   teaspoons
     baking powder
½   teaspoon salt
¾   cup sugar
½   cup whole milk
1   teaspoon pure
     vanilla extract
2   large eggs
¾   cup marshmallow cream

1 Preheat the oven to 350°. Line a 12-cup muffin pan with paper liners. Toss the chocolate chips with 2 teaspoons flour in a small bowl; set aside.

2 Microwave the butter in a separate small microwave-safe bowl until melted. Add the remaining flour, the graham cracker crumbs, baking powder and salt to a large bowl and whisk to combine. Combine the melted butter, sugar, milk, vanilla and eggs in a medium bowl and whisk until smooth. Add the butter mixture to the flour mixture and stir with a rubber spatula until just combined. Add the chocolate chip mixture and stir with the spatula.

3 Pour the batter into the muffin cups with a small ladle or measuring cup, filling them three-quarters of the way. Tap the bottom of the pan lightly against the counter to smooth out the batter. Carefully place in the oven and bake until the muffins are lightly browned and a toothpick inserted into the centers comes out clean, 20 to 25 minutes. Remove the pan from the oven with oven mitts and place on it a wire rack to cool for 5 minutes. Remove the muffins from the pan and place on the rack to cool completely.

4 Spoon 1 tablespoon marshmallow cream onto each muffin. Let set 10 minutes.

Did You Know?

The first printed recipe for s'mores appeared in a Girl Scout guidebook in 1927, when the treats were called Some Mores.

PB&J Muffins

ACTIVE: 35 min   TOTAL: 1 hr (plus cooling)   MAKES: 12

FOR THE MUFFINS

- 6 tablespoons unsalted butter, cut into pieces
- ⅔ cup whole-wheat flour
- ⅔ cup all-purpose flour
- 1 tablespoon baking powder
- ½ teaspoon salt
- ⅓ cup creamy peanut butter
- 1 cup whole milk
- ½ cup packed light brown sugar
- 1 teaspoon pure vanilla extract
- 2 large eggs

FOR THE TOPPINGS

- ⅔ cup creamy peanut butter
- ¾ cup honey-roasted peanuts
- 1 cup strawberry or grape jelly or jam

Tip

When you measure brown sugar, you should firmly press the sugar into your measuring cup to get rid of any air pockets. You don't need to do this with other kinds of sugar.

1 Make the muffins: Preheat the oven to 350°. Line a 12-cup muffin pan with paper liners.

2 Microwave the butter in a small microwave-safe bowl until melted. Add the whole-wheat flour, all-purpose flour, baking powder and salt to a large bowl and whisk to combine. Combine the melted butter, peanut butter, milk, brown sugar, vanilla and eggs in a medium bowl and whisk until smooth. Add the peanut butter mixture to the flour mixture and stir with a rubber spatula until just combined.

3 Pour the batter into the muffin cups with a small ladle or measuring cup, filling them three-quarters of the way. Tap the bottom of the pan lightly against the counter to smooth out the batter. Carefully place in the oven and bake until the muffins are lightly browned and a toothpick inserted into the centers comes out clean, about 25 minutes. Remove the pan from the oven with oven mitts and place it on a wire rack to cool for 5 minutes. Remove the muffins from the pan and place on the rack to cool completely.

4 Make the toppings: Using a teaspoon, scoop out a shallow hole in the middle of each muffin. Microwave the peanut butter in a small microwave-safe bowl, stirring with a spoon halfway through, until loose, 45 to 60 seconds.

5 Finely chop the peanuts with a chef's knife and spread on a plate. Dip the top of a muffin in the melted peanut butter, letting the excess drip off, then dip it in the chopped peanuts to coat. Place on the rack and repeat with the remaining muffins.

6 Spoon 1 heaping tablespoon jelly or jam into the hole in each muffin. Let set 5 minutes.

French Toast Muffins

ACTIVE: 15 min   TOTAL: 40 min   MAKES: 12

Preheat the oven to 350°. Coat a 12-cup muffin pan with **cooking spray.** Combine 2 cups **milk,** 4 **eggs,** ¼ cup **sugar,** 1 tablespoon **vanilla** and ½ teaspoon **nutmeg** in a large bowl and whisk until smooth. Add 8 cups cubed **white bread** and let soak, stirring occasionally, 10 minutes. Spoon the bread mixture into the muffin cups and sprinkle with **sliced almonds.** Bake until set, about 25 minutes. Remove the pan from the oven with oven mitts and place on a wire rack to cool slightly. Remove the muffins from the pan. Serve with **maple syrup.**

Hash Brown Nests

ACTIVE: 15 min   TOTAL: 1 hr   MAKES: 12

Preheat the oven to 400°. Coat a 12-cup muffin pan with **cooking spray.** Thaw 1 pound **frozen shredded potatoes** in a large bowl. Add 4 tablespoons melted **butter,** ½ teaspoon **kosher salt** and a few grinds of **pepper** and stir. Press into the bottom and up the sides of the muffin cups with your fingers. Bake until browned, 45 to 50 minutes. Remove the pan from the oven with oven mitts and let cool slightly. Remove the hash brown nests from the pan and fill with scrambled eggs.

Bacon and Egg Cups

ACTIVE: 10 min   TOTAL: 25 min   MAKES: 6

Preheat the oven to 350°. Cut a single line from the center to the edge of 6 **Canadian bacon slices** using a paring knife. Press each slice, overlapping as needed, into each cup of a 6-cup muffin pan. Crack 1 **egg** into each cup and season with **salt** and **pepper.** Bake until the egg whites are set, 12 to 14 minutes. Remove the pan from the oven with oven mitts and let cool slightly. Remove the egg cups from the pan.

Tip
When you spray your pans with cooking spray, do it over the sink or a trash can so the spray won't get all over the counter.

Cranberry Oatmeal Bites

ACTIVE: 15 min   TOTAL: 40 min   MAKES: 12

Preheat the oven to 350°. Coat a 12-cup muffin pan with **cooking spray.** Combine 1½ cups warm **milk,** 4 tablespoons melted **butter,** ¼ cup **brown sugar,** 2 **eggs,** ½ teaspoon **cinnamon** and a pinch of **salt** in a large bowl and whisk until smooth. Add 3 cups **rolled oats,** ¾ cup each **dried cranberries** and **pepitas** (pumpkin seeds) and ½ teaspoon **baking powder;** stir with a rubber spatula. Spoon into the muffin cups. Bake until set, about 25 minutes. Remove the pan from the oven with oven mitts and place on a wire rack to cool slightly. Remove the oatmeal bites from the pan.

Bacon-Cheddar Wafflewich

ACTIVE: 20 min   TOTAL: 20 min   MAKES: 1

2   slices bacon

2   slices cheddar cheese

2   frozen waffles,
     thawed but not toasted

1   tablespoon unsalted
     butter

Pure maple syrup,
     for serving

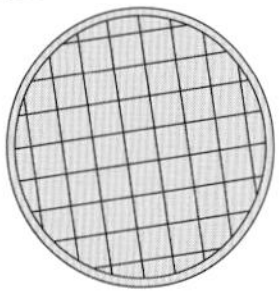

1 Lay the bacon in a medium skillet and cook over medium-high heat, turning occasionally with tongs or a spatula, until the bacon is crisp, about 8 minutes. Remove the bacon with the tongs or spatula and place on paper towels to drain. Remove the skillet from the heat. Bunch up another paper towel and hold it with tongs to wipe out the skillet.

2 Place 1 slice of cheese on a waffle. Top with the bacon, the other slice of cheese and the other waffle to make a sandwich.

3 Melt the butter in the skillet over medium-low heat. Add the waffle sandwich and cook, flipping with a spatula, until golden and the cheese melts, 3 to 5 minutes per side. Remove to a plate and serve with maple syrup.

Did You Know?

Eggo waffles were originally called Froffles—a combination of "frozen" and "waffles." The name clearly didn't stick!

Microwave Frittata

ACTIVE: 5 min   TOTAL: 5 min   MAKES: 1

2   large eggs
1   tablespoon milk
¼   cup shredded mozzarella cheese
2   tablespoons chopped tomato
Kosher salt and freshly ground pepper

1   Combine the eggs and milk in a microwave-safe mug and lightly beat with a fork. Add the cheese and tomato, season with salt and pepper and stir until combined.

2   Microwave, stirring every 20 seconds with a spoon, until the eggs are just set, about 1 minute.

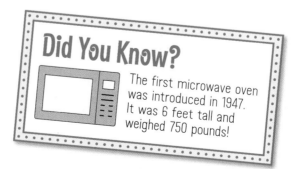

Did You Know?

The first microwave oven was introduced in 1947. It was 6 feet tall and weighed 750 pounds!

Waffle Egg-in-a-Hole

ACTIVE: 15 min   TOTAL: 15 min   MAKES: 1

1   frozen waffle, thawed
    but not toasted

1   large egg

1   tablespoon unsalted
    butter

Kosher salt and freshly
    ground pepper

Pure maple syrup,
    for topping

1   Preheat the oven to 375°. Cut out a 2-inch hole from the center
    of the waffle with a cookie cutter or small drinking glass.

2   Crack the egg into a small bowl or ramekin. Melt the butter in
    a small ovenproof nonstick skillet over medium heat. Add the
    waffle and cook until toasted on the bottom, 2 to 3 minutes.
    Flip with a spatula. Carefully pour the egg into the hole in the
    waffle and season with salt and pepper. Cook until the egg white
    starts to set, about 2 minutes.

3   Carefully put the skillet in the oven and bake until the egg white
    is set but the yolk is still a little runny, about 4 minutes. Remove
    the skillet from the oven with oven mitts and remove the waffle
    to a plate with the spatula. Top with maple syrup.

Tip

Crack your eggs into a
small bowl before you add
them to a dish—that way
you can fish out any bits
of shell if necessary.

Did You Know?

Maple syrup comes
from the sap
of maple trees. It
takes 40 gallons of
sap to make just
one gallon of syrup!

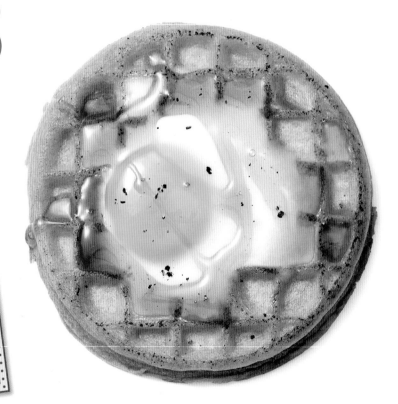

Doughnut Egg-in-a-Hole

ACTIVE: 15 min   TOTAL: 15 min   MAKES: 1

1   large egg
1   tablespoon unsalted
     butter
1   glazed doughnut
Kosher salt and freshly
ground pepper

Tip
If your doughnut's hole is too small for the egg, use a round cookie cutter or a small drinking glass to cut a bigger hole.

1 Preheat the oven to 375°. Crack the egg into a small bowl or ramekin. Melt the butter in a small ovenproof nonstick skillet over medium heat. Add the doughnut and cook until toasted on the bottom, 2 to 3 minutes. Flip with a spatula. Carefully pour the egg into the hole in the doughnut; season with salt and pepper. Cook until the egg white starts to set, about 2 minutes.

2 Carefully put the skillet in the oven and bake until the egg white is set but the yolk is still a little runny, about 4 minutes. Remove the skillet from the oven with oven mitts and remove the doughnut to a plate with the spatula.

Did You Know?

National Doughnut Day, the first Friday in June, was started in 1938 to honor Salvation Army volunteers who served the pastry to US soldiers during World War I.

Almond Butter–Berry Toast

ACTIVE: 10 min   TOTAL: 10 min   MAKES: 4

Toast 4 slices **multigrain bread** in a toaster. Combine ½ cup **raspberries,** ½ cup **blueberries,** 1 teaspoon **lemon juice** and 1 teaspoon chopped **mint** in a small bowl and gently mix with a spoon. Spread **almond butter** on the toast slices with a butter knife. Top with the berry mixture and drizzle with **honey.**

Grape Jelly–Pecan Toast

ACTIVE: 5 min   TOTAL: 5 min   MAKES: 4

Toast 4 slices **multigrain bread** in a toaster. Spread butter on the toast slices with a butter knife, then spread with **grape jelly.** Top with chopped toasted **pecans** and sprinkle with **sea salt.**

Maple-Bacon-Blueberry Toast

ACTIVE: 10 min TOTAL: 10 min MAKES: 4

Toast 4 slices **sourdough bread** in a toaster. Combine 3 ounces softened **cream cheese** with 1½ tablespoons **pure maple syrup** in a small bowl and mix with a spoon until combined; spread on the toast slices with a butter knife. Top with **blueberries** and crumbled cooked **bacon** and drizzle with more maple syrup.

Did You Know?
The toaster was invented before presliced bread. The first pop-up toaster oven came along in 1919; presliced loaves showed up 9 years later!

Chocolate-Banana-Bacon Toast

ACTIVE: 10 min TOTAL: 10 min MAKES: 4

Toast 4 slices **pumpernickel bread** in a toaster. Spread **chocolate-hazelnut spread** on the toast slices with a butter knife. Top with sliced **bananas** and crumbled cooked **bacon** and drizzle with **honey.**

POP QUIZ
Name That Cereal!

See how many of these classics you can ID.

A

B

C

D

E

F

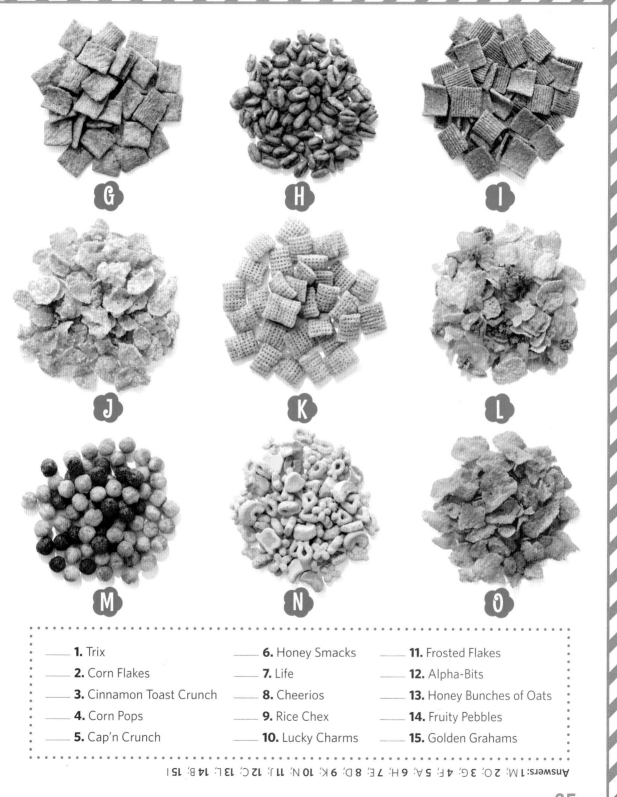

G

H

I

J

K

L

M

N

O

___ **1.** Trix

___ **2.** Corn Flakes

___ **3.** Cinnamon Toast Crunch

___ **4.** Corn Pops

___ **5.** Cap'n Crunch

___ **6.** Honey Smacks

___ **7.** Life

___ **8.** Cheerios

___ **9.** Rice Chex

___ **10.** Lucky Charms

___ **11.** Frosted Flakes

___ **12.** Alpha-Bits

___ **13.** Honey Bunches of Oats

___ **14.** Fruity Pebbles

___ **15.** Golden Grahams

Add apples to a ham and cheese sandwich on page 41!

Lunch

Raisin-Walnut Grilled Cheese

ACTIVE: **10 min**   TOTAL: **10 min**   MAKES: **1**

1   tablespoon cream cheese, at room temperature
1   tablespoon goat cheese, at room temperature
1   teaspoon chopped walnuts
1   teaspoon pure maple syrup
2   slices cinnamon-raisin bread
1   tablespoon unsalted butter, plus more if needed

1   Mix the cream cheese, goat cheese, walnuts and maple syrup in a small bowl with a rubber spatula.

2   Spread the cream cheese mixture on the bread slices and sandwich them together.

3   Melt the butter in a nonstick skillet over medium-low heat. Carefully add the sandwich and cook, flipping once with a spatula, until golden brown and the cheese mixture softens, 2 to 3 minutes per side. Add more butter to the skillet when you flip the sandwich, if needed.

French Grilled Cheese

ACTIVE: **10 min**   TOTAL: **10 min**   MAKES: **1**

1   croissant
1   tablespoon dijonnaise
2   slices muenster cheese
1   thin slice deli ham
1   tablespoon unsalted butter, at room temperature

1   Carefully split open the croissant with a serrated knife. Spread the dijonnaise on the cut sides.

2   Layer 1 slice of cheese, the ham and another slice of cheese on the bottom half of the croissant. Cover with the top half of the croissant. Spread the butter all over the outside of the sandwich.

3   Heat a small nonstick skillet over medium-low heat until hot. Carefully add the sandwich and press it down with the bottom of another skillet. Leave the skillet in place and cook the sandwich, flipping it once with a spatula, until golden brown and the cheese melts, about 3 minutes per side.

Pizza Grilled Cheese

ACTIVE: **10 min**   TOTAL: **10 min**   MAKES: **1**

1 **tablespoon tomato sauce**
2 **slices sourdough bread**
2 **tablespoons shredded mozzarella cheese**
1 **tablespoon grated parmesan cheese**
3 **basil leaves**
1 **tablespoon unsalted butter, plus more if needed**

1 Spread the tomato sauce on 1 slice of bread. Top with the mozzarella, parmesan, basil and the other slice of bread.

2 Melt the butter in a small nonstick skillet over medium-low heat. Carefully add the sandwich and cook, flipping it once with a spatula, until golden brown and the cheese melts, 3 to 4 minutes per side. Add more butter to the skillet when you flip the sandwich, if needed.

Tip
Try cooking your grilled cheese in a waffle iron—it will get nice and crispy, and it'll look cool, too!

Hoagie Grilled Cheese

ACTIVE: **10 min**   TOTAL: **10 min**   MAKES: **1**

1 **hoagie roll**
2 **slices provolone cheese**
4 **thin slices salami**
1 **tablespoon chopped hot cherry peppers or roasted red peppers**
1 **tablespoon extra-virgin olive oil**

1 Carefully split the roll in half lengthwise with a serrated knife.

2 Layer 1 slice of cheese, the salami, hot cherry peppers and the other slice of cheese on the bottom half of the roll. Cover with the top half of the roll.

3 Heat the olive oil in a small nonstick skillet over medium-low heat. Carefully add the sandwich and press it down with the bottom of another skillet. Leave the skillet in place and cook the sandwich, flipping it once with a spatula, until golden brown and the cheese melts, 3 to 4 minutes per side.

Ham and Cheese Wafflewiches with Kale Chips

ACTIVE: **30 min**   TOTAL: **30 min**   MAKES: **4**

FOR THE KALE CHIPS

1   bunch Tuscan kale (about 1 pound)

1   tablespoon extra-virgin olive oil

Kosher salt

FOR THE SANDWICHES

1   Granny Smith apple, peeled and grated on the large holes of a box grater

⅓   cup honey mustard

8   frozen waffles

½   pound sliced deli ham

¼   pound sliced cheddar cheese

2   tablespoons unsalted butter, plus more if needed

1   Make the kale chips: Preheat the oven to 275°. Carefully cut off the tough stems of the kale with a chef's knife; discard. Chop the kale leaves into 1½-inch pieces. Toss the kale on a baking sheet with the olive oil and ½ teaspoon salt and spread in a single layer.

2   Bake the kale for 10 minutes, then remove the baking sheet from the oven with oven mitts and flip the kale leaves with tongs or a spatula. Put back in the oven and continue to bake until the kale leaves are crisp, about 10 more minutes.

3   Meanwhile, make the sandwiches: Stir together the grated apple with the honey mustard in a medium bowl until combined. Spoon the apple mixture on 4 waffles and spread evenly. Top with the ham, cheese and remaining waffles to make 4 sandwiches.

4   Melt the butter in a large nonstick skillet over medium heat. Carefully add the sandwiches and cook, flipping once with a spatula, until golden, about 3 minutes per side. Add more butter to the skillet when you flip the sandwich, if needed. Serve with the kale chips.

Tip

If you decide to use a different cheese, make sure you choose a good melter: Cheddar, American, provolone and muenster are some of the best.

Dried
Cranberry-
Grape

Chicken Salad

Roasted
Red Pepper-
Cucumber

Avocado-Bacon

❶ Pick Your Mix-Ins

Choose up to 3 of these ingredients and combine to make 1 cup total.

Celery, diced

Carrots, diced

Seedless grapes, halved

Apple, diced

Cucumber, diced

Roasted red peppers, diced

Avocado, diced

Red, white or sweet onion, diced (up to ¼ cup)

Raisins or dried cranberries

Cooked bacon, crumbled

Toasted nuts, chopped

Corn kernels

❷ Mix the Dressing

Combine 2 teaspoons lemon juice or apple cider vinegar, 1 teaspoon dijon mustard, ½ teaspoon kosher salt and a few grinds of pepper in a large bowl and whisk until smooth. Stir in ⅔ cup of one of the following until smooth.

Mayonnaise

Mayonnaise and sour cream (⅓ cup of each)

Plain yogurt

❸ Make the Salad

Add 4 cups chopped or shredded rotisserie chicken (skin removed) to the bowl with the dressing. Add your mix-ins. Season with salt and pepper and stir to coat.

❹ Add Extra Flavor

Choose 1 or 2 of these ingredients, chop and combine to make 2 tablespoons total. Add to the chicken salad and mix well.

Parsley   Chives   Cilantro   Basil   Dill   Fresh or pickled jalapeño

Pesto Pizza English Muffin

ACTIVE: **10 min**   TOTAL: **10 min**   SERVES: **1**

¼   cup part-skim ricotta cheese
1   tablespoon pesto
Kosher salt and freshly ground pepper
1   English muffin, split
2   tablespoons shredded Italian cheese blend
Chopped fresh basil, for topping

1   Preheat the broiler. Mix together the ricotta and pesto in a small bowl. Season with salt and pepper.

2   Toast the English muffin in a toaster. Spread the ricotta mixture on the cut sides of the English muffin. Sprinkle with the shredded cheese.

3   Place the English muffin halves on a baking sheet, carefully place under the broiler and broil until the cheese is browned and bubbling, about 3 minutes. Top with basil.

Buffalo Chicken English Muffin

ACTIVE: **10 min**   TOTAL: **10 min**   SERVES: **1**

1   tablespoon mayonnaise
1   tablespoon sour cream
1   tablespoon Buffalo hot sauce
½   cup shredded rotisserie chicken (skin removed)
Kosher salt
1   English muffin, split
Unsalted butter, at room temperature, for spreading
Finely chopped celery and carrots, for topping

1   Mix together the mayonnaise, sour cream and hot sauce in a small bowl. Stir in the chicken and season with salt.

2   Toast the English muffin in a toaster. Spread butter on the cut sides of the English muffin and top with the chicken salad and some celery and carrots.

Curried Tuna Melt English Muffin

ACTIVE: **10 min**   TOTAL: **10 min**   SERVES: **1**

2   tablespoons mayonnaise
½   teaspoon curry powder
1   3-ounce can tuna, drained
1   scallion, thinly sliced
Kosher salt and freshly ground pepper
1   English muffin, split
2   small slices cheddar cheese
Sweet potato chips, for topping

1   Preheat the broiler. Mix together the mayonnaise and curry powder in a small bowl. Stir in the tuna and scallion. Season with salt and pepper.

2   Toast the English muffin in a toaster. Spread the tuna mixture on the cut sides of the English muffin. Top each half with a slice of cheese.

3   Place the English muffin halves on a baking sheet, carefully place under the broiler and broil until the cheese is melted, about 3 minutes. Top with sweet potato chips.

Tex-Mex English Muffin

ACTIVE: **10 min**   TOTAL: **10 min**   SERVES: **1**

1   English muffin, split
2   tablespoons refried beans
2   tablespoons shredded pepper jack cheese
Salsa, sour cream, chopped pickled jalapeños and fresh cilantro, for topping

1   Preheat the broiler. Toast the English muffin in a toaster. Spread the beans on the cut sides of the English muffin and top with the cheese.

2   Place the English muffin halves on a baking sheet, carefully place under the broiler and broil until the cheese is melted, about 3 minutes. Top with salsa, sour cream, pickled jalapeños and cilantro.

Tip
Split English muffins in half with a fork, not a knife, so you'll end up with good nooks and crannies.

Fresh Tomato Soup with Grilled Ham and Cheese

ACTIVE: **30 min**   TOTAL: **35 min**   SERVES: **4**

FOR THE SOUP

4½ pounds tomatoes

1½ tablespoons extra-virgin olive oil

1   clove garlic, minced

2   scallions, chopped

1½ tablespoons heavy cream

Kosher salt and freshly ground pepper

½   cup mini bow ties or other mini pasta

Chopped fresh basil, for topping

FOR THE SANDWICHES

½   cup shredded part-skim mozzarella cheese

½   cup shredded sharp cheddar cheese

2   scallions, chopped

4   slices multigrain bread

2   thin slices low-sodium deli ham

½   tablespoon extra-virgin olive oil

1 Make the soup: Carefully cut 4 pounds of the tomatoes into quarters with a serrated knife and chop the rest. Put the quartered tomatoes in a blender and puree until smooth.

2 Heat the olive oil in a large pot over medium heat. Add the garlic and scallions and cook, stirring with a wooden spoon, 2 minutes.

3 Increase the heat to medium high. Hold a fine-mesh sieve over the pot and strain the pureed tomatoes into the pot. Stir in the chopped tomatoes, 1 cup water, the heavy cream, ½ teaspoon salt and ¼ teaspoon pepper. Bring to a simmer and cook until thickened, about 5 minutes.

4 Add the pasta to the soup and cook until tender, about 10 minutes. Season with salt and pepper.

5 Meanwhile, make the sandwiches: Toss the cheeses with the scallions in a medium bowl. Sprinkle half the mixture on 2 slices of bread. Top each with a slice of ham, the remaining cheese mixture and the other 2 slices of bread.

6 Heat the olive oil in a large nonstick skillet over medium-low heat. Carefully add the sandwiches and cook, flipping once with a spatula, until the cheese melts, about 3 minutes per side.

7 Ladle the soup into bowls and top with basil. Serve each bowl with a sandwich half.

Tip
Bruised or imperfect tomatoes are great for making soup. Just be sure your tomatoes aren't rotten: If they're leaking liquid or show signs of mold, you should toss them.

Taco Salad Cups

ACTIVE: **10 min**   TOTAL: **20 min**   MAKES: **6**

Cooking spray

6   **6-inch flour tortillas**

Kosher salt

Chili powder, to taste

¾   **cup refried beans**

¾   **cup guacamole**

Sour cream, fresh salsa, cilantro and shredded lettuce and cheddar, for topping

1 Preheat the oven to 425°. Coat a 6-cup jumbo muffin pan with cooking spray. Press 1 tortilla into each cup, pleating it to make it fit. Lightly coat the tortillas with cooking spray and season each with salt and a pinch of chili powder.

2 Bake the tortilla cups until golden, 8 to 10 minutes. Remove from the oven using oven mitts, place the muffin pan on a rack and let the tortilla cups cool completely.

3 Carefully remove the tortilla cups from the muffin pan. Divide the beans and guacamole among the cups. Top each with sour cream, salsa, cilantro, lettuce and cheese.

Tip

You'll need a jumbo-muffin pan for these; regular muffin pans are too small. If you don't have one, you can bake the taco cups in small ovenproof bowls.

Did You Know?

In 2018, more than 350 people in Tancítaro, Michoacán, Mexico, made the world's largest serving of guacamole: It weighed 8,351 pounds!

Cuban Beef Pockets

ACTIVE: **25 min**   TOTAL: **50 min**   SERVES: **4**

2   teaspoons vegetable oil, plus more for brushing

1   shallot, finely chopped

1   clove garlic, minced

Pinch of ground cinnamon

½   pound ground beef

Kosher salt and freshly ground pepper

1   tablespoon tomato paste

3   tablespoons chopped tomato

3   tablespoons golden raisins

3   large pimiento-stuffed olives, finely chopped

All-purpose flour, for dusting

1   11-ounce tube refrigerated French bread dough

1   large egg

Tip
"Egg wash" is egg beaten with water, milk or cream. Brushing it on dough before baking gives the crust a shiny look.

1 Heat the vegetable oil in a medium skillet over medium-high heat. Add the shallot, garlic and cinnamon and cook, stirring with a wooden spoon, 1 minute.

2 Add the beef, ¼ teaspoon salt and a few grinds of pepper. Cook, breaking up the meat with the wooden spoon, until browned, about 3 minutes.

3 Add the tomato paste, chopped tomato, raisins and olives to the skillet and cook, stirring to coat, 2 minutes. Season with salt and pepper. Remove from the heat and let the beef mixture cool completely.

4 Preheat the oven to 425°. Lightly brush a baking sheet with vegetable oil. Lightly dust your work surface with flour. Cut the French bread dough into 4 equal pieces. Using a rolling pin, roll out each piece of dough on the floured surface into a 6-by-8-inch rectangle.

5 Divide the beef mixture among the dough rectangles, piling it in the center. Fold the 2 shorter sides of the dough over the filling, stretching the dough to cover. Fold in the 2 long sides to enclose. Pinch the seams with your fingers to seal.

6 Move the pockets seam-side down to the oiled baking sheet. Beat the egg and 1 tablespoon water with a fork in a small bowl. Brush the pockets with the egg wash. Bake until golden brown, about 15 minutes. Remove from the oven using oven mitts and let cool slightly.

Curried Chicken Pockets

ACTIVE: **25 min**   TOTAL: **50 min**   SERVES: **4**

- 1 **tablespoon vegetable oil, plus more for brushing**
- 1 **shallot, finely chopped**
- ¾ **teaspoon curry powder**
- ½ **teaspoon grated peeled fresh ginger**
- 1 **clove garlic, grated**
- 1 **cup shredded rotisserie chicken (skin removed)**
- ¼ **cup frozen peas, thawed**
- ¼ **cup plain low-fat yogurt**
- 2 **tablespoons chopped fresh cilantro**
- 1 **teaspoon fresh lime juice**

Kosher salt

All-purpose flour, for dusting

- 1 **11-ounce tube refrigerated French bread dough**
- 1 **large egg**

1 Heat the vegetable oil in a medium skillet over medium heat. Add the shallot, curry powder, ginger and garlic and cook, stirring with a wooden spoon, until the shallot is slightly softened, about 2 minutes. Stir in the chicken. Remove the skillet from the heat.

2 Stir the peas, yogurt, cilantro and lime juice into the chicken mixture. Season with salt. Let the chicken mixture cool completely.

3 Preheat the oven to 425°. Lightly brush a baking sheet with vegetable oil. Lightly dust your work surface with flour. Cut the French bread dough into 4 equal pieces. Using a rolling pin, roll out each piece of dough on the floured surface into a 6-by-8-inch rectangle.

4 Divide the chicken mixture among the dough rectangles, piling it in the center. Fold the 2 shorter sides of the dough over the filling, stretching the dough to cover. Fold in the 2 long sides to enclose. Pinch the seams with your fingers to seal.

5 Move the pockets seam-side down to the oiled baking sheet. Beat the egg and 1 tablespoon water with a fork in a small bowl. Brush the pockets with the egg wash. Bake until golden brown, about 15 minutes. Remove from the oven using oven mitts and let cool slightly.

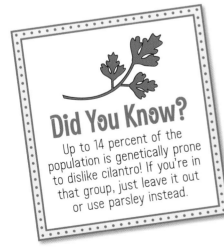

Did You Know?

Up to 14 percent of the population is genetically prone to dislike cilantro! If you're in that group, just leave it out or use parsley instead.

Ham and Cheese Noodle Salad

ACTIVE: **20 min**   TOTAL: **25 min**   SERVES: **4**

Kosher salt

12 ounces multigrain spaghetti

3   tablespoons red wine vinegar

2   tablespoons low-fat plain yogurt

2   teaspoons dijon mustard

2   scallions, thinly sliced

1   tablespoon chopped fresh dill (optional)

Freshly ground pepper

3   tablespoons extra-virgin olive oil

1   green bell pepper, thinly sliced

2   ounces sliced deli ham, cut into strips

2   ounces sliced cheddar cheese, cut into strips

½   small head romaine lettuce, thinly sliced

1 Fill a large pot with water and season with salt. Bring to a boil over high heat. Add the spaghetti and cook as the label directs for al dente. Carefully drain the spaghetti in a colander set in the sink. Rinse the spaghetti in the colander under cold water until cool.

2 Make the dressing: Combine the vinegar, yogurt, mustard, scallions, dill and ½ teaspoon salt in a large bowl and whisk until smooth; season with pepper. Drizzle in the olive oil, while whisking, until combined.

3 Add the spaghetti, bell pepper, ham, cheese and lettuce to the dressing and toss to combine.

Did You Know?

"Spaghetti" comes from the Italian word *spago*, which means string. If you wanted a single piece of spaghetti in Italy, you'd say spaghetto—but who ever wants just one piece?

Tip

Be sure to use plain yogurt for this dressing. Vanilla or other flavored yogurts would be way too sweet!

POP QUIZ

Lunch-Box
Close-Ups

Take a really close look at these foods. Can you tell what they are?

1 _____

2 _____

3 _____

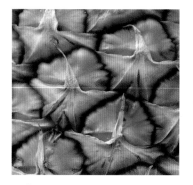

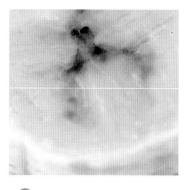

4 _____

5 _____

6 _____

7 _____

8 _____

9 _____

10 _____

11 _____

12 _____

13 _____

14 _____

15 _____

Make a fun popcorn mix! See page 70.

56

Snacks

Raspberry Applesauce

ACTIVE: 15 min   TOTAL: 40 min   MAKES: about 2 cups

2 **pounds assorted apples (such as Golden Delicious, Gala and McIntosh; about 4), peeled and chopped**

2 **tablespoons sugar**

Juice of ½ lemon

1 **cup raspberries**

1 Combine the apples, sugar and ½ cup water in a medium saucepan. Bring to a simmer over medium-high heat, stirring occasionally. Reduce the heat to medium; cover and cook until the apples are very soft and most of the liquid has evaporated, about 20 minutes.

2 Add the lemon juice to the apples. Carefully pour into a blender or food processor and puree (or puree in the pan with an immersion blender). Put the applesauce in a bowl and stir in the raspberries, slightly mashing them with a fork. Refrigerate until cool.

Tip
You can make this applesauce in the microwave: Put the apples, sugar and water in a large microwave-safe bowl, cover and microwave 10 minutes. Uncover and continue with step 2.

Strawberries with Yogurt Dip

ACTIVE: 5 min   TOTAL: 5 min   SERVES: 1

1   **cup low-fat plain Greek yogurt**

3   **tablespoons strawberry preserves**

¼   **teaspoon pure vanilla extract**

¼   **teaspoon ground cinnamon**

6   **strawberries, stems removed**

1 Put the yogurt in a small bowl. Add the strawberry preserves, vanilla and cinnamon and stir until swirled.

2 Thread the strawberries onto wooden skewers. Serve with the dip.

Did You Know?

Strawberries are one of the only fruits with seeds on the outside. The average strawberry has about 200 seeds!

Candied Grapes

ACTIVE: **15 min**   TOTAL: **35 min**   SERVES: **4**

1 **3-ounce package grape gelatin powder**

2 **cups red seedless grapes**

1 Sprinkle the gelatin powder on a rimmed baking sheet. Soak the grapes in a bowl of cold water. Remove a few of the grapes with a slotted spoon and put on the baking sheet; roll the grapes in the gelatin powder until coated. Place the coated grapes on a plate.

2 Repeat the process to coat the remaining grapes in small batches. Let dry, about 20 minutes.

Tip
You can use any flavor of gelatin for these grapes, like lemon, watermelon or raspberry— the coating just won't be purple!

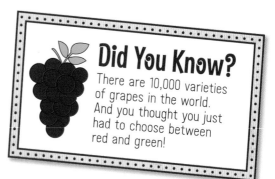

Did You Know?
There are 10,000 varieties of grapes in the world. And you thought you just had to choose between red and green!

Sweet Strawberry Popcorn

ACTIVE: 10 min   TOTAL: 10 min   SERVES: 4 to 6

1   **cup freeze-dried strawberries**

3   **tablespoons confectioners' sugar**

2   **tablespoons unsalted butter**

8   **cups popcorn**

½   **cup white chocolate chips**

1 Combine ½ cup freeze-dried strawberries and the confectioners' sugar in a mini food processor and pulse until powdery.

2 Microwave the butter in a small microwave-safe bowl until melted. Put the popcorn in a large bowl. Drizzle the melted butter over the popcorn and sprinkle with the strawberry sugar. Toss until coated.

3 Add the white chocolate chips and the remaining ½ cup freeze-dried strawberries to the popcorn and toss.

Tip
Make a little extra strawberry sugar and sprinkle it on plain yogurt or buttered toast!

Granola Bars

❶ Prepare the Base

Preheat the oven to 350° and line a 9-by-13-inch baking pan with foil, leaving an overhang; coat with cooking spray and set aside. Toss 3 cups rolled oats with 2 tablespoons vegetable oil or melted butter on a rimmed baking sheet and spread in a single layer. Bake until toasted, 18 to 20 minutes. Let cool completely on the baking sheet, then scrape into a large bowl. Stir in 1 cup of the following (choose one or a combination).

| Salted roasted nuts (any kind), chopped | Salted roasted sunflower seeds | Salted roasted pepitas | Toasted shredded coconut (sweetened or unsweetened) |

❷ Choose Your Mix-Ins

Measure out 1 cup of the following (choose one or a combination); set aside.

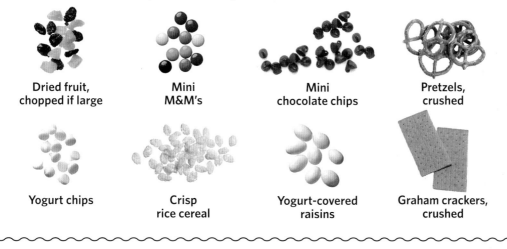

Dried fruit, chopped if large   Mini M&M's   Mini chocolate chips   Pretzels, crushed

Yogurt chips   Crisp rice cereal   Yogurt-covered raisins   Graham crackers, crushed

❸ Make the Bars

Combine 6 tablespoons unsalted butter (or 2 tablespoons each coconut oil and vegetable oil) in a medium saucepan with ½ cup light brown sugar, 1 teaspoon vanilla and 1 teaspoon salt. Bring to a boil over medium heat, stirring occasionally. (The mixture will bubble and foam.) Cook just 30 seconds, then carefully pour over the oat mixture and stir with a rubber spatula. Let cool slightly, then stir in your mix-ins. Pour into the prepared 9-by-13-inch pan and press firmly and evenly with the spatula.

❹ Let Cool

Let the bars stand at room temperature until completely cool and firm enough to slice, 1 to 3 hours. Lift out of the pan using the foil overhang and put on a cutting board; remove the foil. Carefully cut into 24 rectangular bars with a serrated knife. Store in an airtight container at room temperature for up to 5 days.

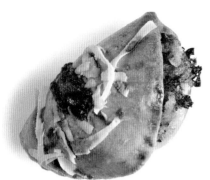

Cheesy Broccoli Pockets

ACTIVE: **20 min**   TOTAL: **40 min**   MAKES: **12**

¼   **cup chopped broccoli florets**
1   **pound pizza dough, at room temperature**
All-purpose flour, for dusting
¼   **cup shredded cheddar cheese**
1   **large egg, beaten**
Shredded parmesan cheese, for topping

1   Preheat the oven to 400˚. Put the broccoli in a microwave-safe bowl. Add 1 tablespoon water. Cover and microwave until the broccoli is tender and bright green, about 2 minutes. Drain and set aside.

2   Using a rolling pin, roll out the pizza dough on a lightly floured surface until ¼ inch thick. Cut into twelve 3-inch rounds with a cookie cutter or small glass. Spoon small scoops of the broccoli and cheese onto each dough round, leaving a small border. Brush the edges with the beaten egg, fold in half and gently press the edges with your fingers or a fork to seal. Brush with more beaten egg and sprinkle with parmesan.

3   Line a baking sheet with parchment paper. Arrange the pockets on the baking sheet and poke a hole in the top of each with a skewer. Bake until golden, about 20 minutes. Let cool slightly.

Pizza Pockets

ACTIVE: **15 min**   TOTAL: **35 min**   MAKES: **12**

1   **pound pizza dough, at room temperature**
All-purpose flour, for dusting
2   **tablespoons tomato sauce**
¼   **cup shredded mozzarella cheese**
2   **tablespoons shredded parmesan cheese**
1   **large egg, beaten**

1   Preheat the oven to 400˚. Using a rolling pin, roll out the pizza dough on a lightly floured surface until ¼ inch thick. Cut into twelve 3-inch rounds with a cookie cutter or small glass.

2   Spread small spoonfuls of tomato sauce onto each dough round, leaving a small border. Top with the mozzarella and parmesan. Brush the edges with the beaten egg, fold in half and gently press the edges with your fingers or a fork to seal. Brush with more beaten egg and sprinkle with more parmesan.

3   Line a baking sheet with parchment paper. Arrange the pockets on the baking sheet and poke a hole in the top of each with a skewer. Bake until golden, about 20 minutes. Let cool slightly.

Cinnamon-Apple Pockets

ACTIVE: 15 min   TOTAL: 35 min   MAKES: 12

1   pound pizza dough, at room temperature
All-purpose flour, for dusting
1   teaspoon ground cinnamon
1   teaspoon sugar
¼   cup ricotta cheese
1   apple, diced
1   large egg, beaten

1   Preheat the oven to 400°. Using a rolling pin, roll out the pizza dough on a lightly floured surface until ¼ inch thick. Cut into twelve 3-inch rounds with a cookie cutter or small glass.

2   Mix the cinnamon and sugar together in a small bowl. Spoon small scoops of ricotta onto each dough round, leaving a small border, then top with the apple and a pinch of the cinnamon sugar. Brush the edges with the beaten egg, fold in half and gently press the edges with your fingers or a fork to seal. Brush with more beaten egg and sprinkle with more cinnamon sugar.

3   Line a baking sheet with parchment paper. Arrange the pockets on the baking sheet and poke a hole in the top of each with a skewer. Bake until golden, about 20 minutes. Let cool slightly.

Apricot Jam Pockets

ACTIVE: 15 min   TOTAL: 35 min   MAKES: 12

1   pound pizza dough, at room temperature
All-purpose flour, for dusting
2   ounces cream cheese, at room temperature
2   tablespoons apricot jam
1   large egg, beaten
Sugar, for sprinkling

1   Preheat the oven to 400°. Using a rolling pin, roll out the pizza dough on a lightly floured surface until ¼ inch thick. Cut into twelve 3-inch rounds with a cookie cutter or small glass.

2   Spoon small scoops of cream cheese and apricot jam onto each dough round, leaving a small border. Brush the edges with beaten egg, fold in half and gently press the edges with your fingers or a fork to seal. Brush with more beaten egg and sprinkle with sugar.

3   Line a baking sheet with parchment paper. Arrange the pockets on the baking sheet and poke a hole in the top of each with a skewer. Bake until golden, about 20 minutes. Let cool slightly.

MAKE YOUR OWN **Chips!**

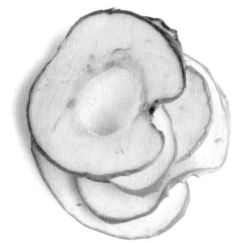

Cinnamon Tortilla Chips

ACTIVE: 10 min   TOTAL: 25 min   SERVES: 6 to 8

Preheat the oven to 375°. Cut 8 **corn tortillas** into wedges with a chef's knife. Toss with **vegetable oil** in a large bowl; sprinkle with **cinnamon sugar.** Lay out in a single layer on 2 baking sheets. Bake until crisp, about 8 minutes per side, carefully flipping with a spatula. Let cool.

Dried Apple Chips

ACTIVE: 10 min   TOTAL: 2 hr 10 min   SERVES: 6 to 8

Preheat the oven to 200°. Brush 2 baking sheets with **vegetable oil.** Cut 3 **apples** in half with a chef's knife. Scoop out the seeds with a spoon. Slice each into ¼-inch-thick rounds. Lay out in a single layer on the baking sheets. Bake until dry, 2 to 3 hours.

Tip

When you're making chips, thinner is better. Ask a grown-up to help you slice the ingredients as thinly as possible.

Sesame Potato Chips

ACTIVE: 10 min   TOTAL: 20 min   SERVES: 6 to 8

Put 2 baking sheets in the oven and preheat to 425°. Thinly slice 3 **russet potatoes** with a chef's knife (or have a grown-up slice the potatoes on a mandoline). Toss with **olive oil** in a large bowl; season with **salt.** Carefully remove the hot baking sheets from the oven with oven mitts and spread the potatoes on the baking sheets. Sprinkle with **sesame seeds.** Bake until the potatoes are crisp and golden, about 10 minutes. Let cool.

Banana Chips

ACTIVE: 10 min   TOTAL: 2½ hr   SERVES: 4 to 6

Preheat the oven to 200°. Brush a baking sheet with **vegetable oil.** Slice 4 **bananas** into ⅛-inch-thick rounds with a paring knife and lay out in a single layer on the baking sheet. Bake until golden, 2 to 3 hours. Let sit at room temperature until firm.

Ants on a Log Remix!

Ants on a Ranch

Celery sticks + cream cheese mixed with ranch dressing + peas

Berries on a Branch

Celery sticks + cookie butter + blueberries

Ladybugs on a Log

Celery sticks + strawberry cream cheese + dried cranberries

Tip

You can create your own version of ants on a log: Just top celery with any spread (like a nut butter or your favorite dip) and something small, like dried fruit or a snack mix. Be sure to name your recipe—that's the fun part!

Beans on a Stalk

Celery sticks + guacamole
+ black beans

Fish in a Stream

Celery sticks + hummus +
Goldfish pretzels

Pigs in a Pen

Celery sticks +
pimiento cheese + bacon

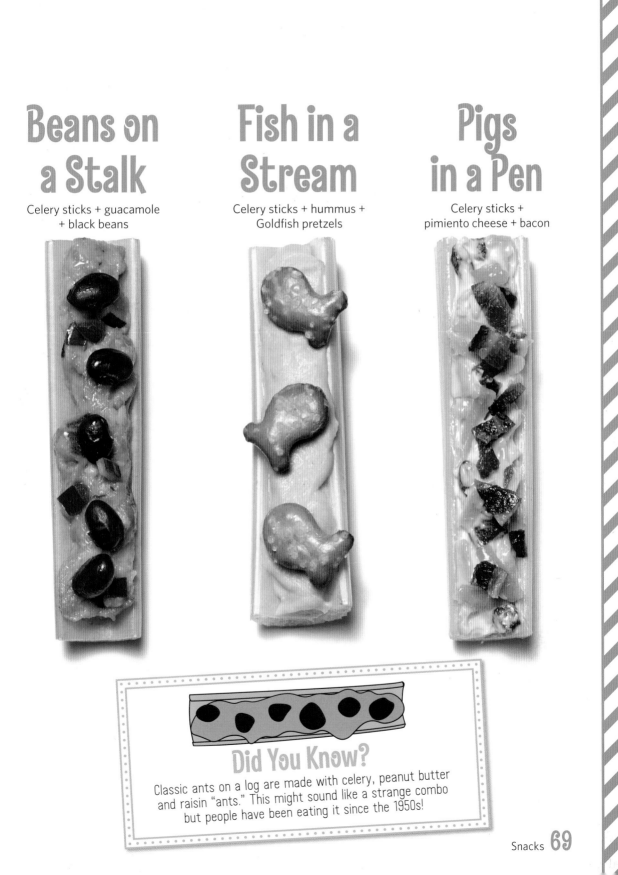

Did You Know?

Classic ants on a log are made with celery, peanut butter and raisin "ants." This might sound like a strange combo but people have been eating it since the 1950s!

Cheesy Chex Mix

ACTIVE: **10 min**   TOTAL: **25 min**   SERVES: **6 to 8**

Preheat the oven to 325°. Microwave 4 tablespoons **butter** in a small microwave-safe bowl until melted. Combine 3 cups **Chex cereal,** 2 cups **mini pretzels,** 1 cup **cheese crackers,** ¾ cup shredded **parmesan,** the melted butter and a pinch of **garlic powder** in a large bowl and toss until combined. Spread on a rimmed baking sheet and bake, carefully stirring with a rubber spatula halfway through, 15 minutes.

Fruity Popcorn Mix

ACTIVE: **10 min**   TOTAL: **15 min**   SERVES: **6 to 8**

Combine 4 cups hot **popcorn** with 2 cups **freeze-dried strawberries** and 1 cup **apple chips** in a large bowl and toss. Sprinkle with a pinch each of **cinnamon** and **salt.**

Pecan Caramel Popcorn

ACTIVE: 10 min   TOTAL: 45 min   SERVES: 6 to 8

Preheat the oven to 325°. Line a baking sheet with parchment paper. Microwave 5 tablespoons **butter** in a small microwave-safe bowl with 1 tablespoon **honey** and a pinch of **salt** until melted. Combine 12 cups **popcorn** and 1 cup **pecans** in a large bowl; drizzle with the butter mixture and toss to coat. Spread on the baking sheet and bake, carefully stirring with a spatula halfway through, 15 minutes. Let cool.

Chocolate-Peanut Puppy Chow

ACTIVE: 10 min   TOTAL: 15 min   SERVES: 6 to 8

Combine 4 tablespoons each **butter, creamy peanut butter** and **chocolate chips** in a small microwave-safe bowl and microwave until melted. Combine 3 cups each **chow mein noodles** and **Chex cereal** and ½ cup each **raisins** and chopped **peanuts** in a large resealable plastic bag. Add the melted chocolate–peanut butter mixture, seal and shake to coat. Open, add 2 cups **confectioners' sugar,** seal and shake again. Let cool.

Tip

Cut your fruits and veggies with a crinkle cutter—it's a knife with a wavy edge. You can also use the cutter for the cake fries on page 172.

Pineapple Fries + Raspberry-Lime Dip

ACTIVE: 10 min   TOTAL: 10 min   SERVES: 4

For the dip, combine 1 cup **sweetened coconut-milk yogurt,** 3 tablespoons **seedless raspberry jam** and ¼ teaspoon grated **lime zest** in a medium bowl and whisk until smooth. Serve with **pineapple sticks.**

Carrot Fries + Red Pepper Hummus

ACTIVE: 10 min   TOTAL: 10 min   SERVES: 4

For the dip, combine ¾ cup canned **chickpeas** (drained and rinsed), ½ cup chopped **roasted red peppers,** 2 tablespoons **tahini,** ½ **garlic clove,** the juice of 1 **lemon,** 1 teaspoon **kosher salt** and ¼ teaspoon **smoked paprika** in a blender and puree until smooth. Serve with **rainbow carrot sticks.**

Jicama Fries + Black Bean Dip

ACTIVE: 10 min   TOTAL: 10 min   SERVES: 4

For the dip, combine ¾ cup canned **refried black beans,** ¼ cup **sour cream,** 2 tablespoons **lime juice** and ¾ teaspoon each **chili powder** and **kosher salt** in a blender and puree until smooth. Serve with **jicama sticks.**

Kohlrabi Fries + Creamy Herb Dip

ACTIVE: **10 min**   TOTAL: **10 min**   SERVES: **4**

For the dip, combine ⅓ cup **sour cream,** 3 tablespoons **dijon mustard,** 1 tablespoon **lemon juice** and ½ teaspoon **kosher salt** in a medium bowl and whisk. Slowly whisk in ½ cup **olive oil.** Stir in 2 tablespoons chopped **parsley.** (If the dip begins to separate, whisk in ½ to 1 teaspoon water until smooth.) Serve with **kohlrabi sticks.**

Apple Fries + Nut Butter Dip

ACTIVE: **10 min**   TOTAL: **10 min**   SERVES: **4**

For the dip, combine 4 ounces softened **cream cheese,** ½ cup **creamy peanut** or **cashew butter,** ¼ cup **brown sugar,** 5 tablespoons **milk** and ½ teaspoon **cinnamon** in a large bowl and beat with a mixer until smooth. Serve with **apple sticks.**

Melon Fries + Honey-Basil Dip

ACTIVE: **10 min**   TOTAL: **10 min**   SERVES: **4**

For the dip, combine 1 cup plain whole-milk **Greek yogurt,** ¼ cup **honey** and 3 tablespoons chopped **basil** in a blender and puree. Serve with **cantaloupe** and **honeydew melon sticks.**

Berry Brownie Bites

ACTIVE: 15 min   TOTAL: 45 min   MAKES: 24

Preheat the oven to 350°. Coat a 24-cup mini-muffin pan with **cooking spray.** Prepare one 18-ounce box **brownie mix** as the label directs. Divide the batter among the mini-muffin cups. Press a **raspberry** or sliced **strawberry** into each cup. Bake until a toothpick inserted into the middle of the brownies comes out almost clean, 15 to 18 minutes. Let cool.

Tip
To eat a mango half, score the flesh in a grid pattern like you see here, then press on the skin side to pop out the cubes!

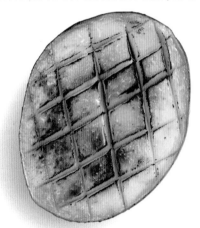

Caramelized Mango

ACTIVE: 10 min   TOTAL: 15 min   SERVES: 2

Carefully slice off the two wide sides of a **mango** with a chef's knife, cutting alongside the pit, then score the flesh in a grid pattern without cutting all the way through the skin. Sprinkle with **sugar** and put on a baking sheet. Broil until lightly charred. Squeeze some **lime juice** over the tops.

Fruit Skewers with Lime Dip

ACTIVE: 10 min   TOTAL: 10 min   SERVES: 4

Combine 1 cup **low-fat sour cream** and 2 tablespoons each **brown sugar** and **lime juice** in a medium bowl and whisk until smooth; sprinkle with **cinnamon sugar.** Thread stemmed **strawberries** and **pineapple chunks** onto skewers; serve with the dip.

Did You Know?

Scientists genetically engineered an apple that won't brown when it's cut. It's called the Arctic apple—keep an eye out for it at the supermarket!

Cheddar-Apple Skewers

ACTIVE: 10 min   TOTAL: 10 min   SERVES: 4

Carefully cut 6 ounces **cheddar cheese** into bite-size cubes with a chef's knife. Cut 2 **apples** into bite-size cubes and toss with **lemon juice.** Thread the cheddar and apple onto small skewers and drizzle with **honey.**

Baked Mozzarella Sticks

ACTIVE: 10 min   TOTAL: 25 min   MAKES: 8

8   mozzarella cheese
     sticks

¼   cup all-purpose flour

1   large egg

½   cup whole-wheat panko

Warm marinara sauce,
     for serving

1 Unwrap the mozzarella sticks, place on a baking sheet and freeze until firm, about 20 minutes.

2 Preheat the oven to 425°. Line a baking sheet with parchment paper. Remove the mozzarella sticks from the freezer. Put the flour in a shallow bowl. Lightly beat the egg in another bowl. Put the panko in a third bowl.

3 Toss the mozzarella sticks in the flour, then dip in the egg, then roll in the panko to coat. Lay out on the baking sheet and bake until crisp, 6 to 7 minutes. Serve with marinara sauce.

Did You Know?

Cheese makers use about 20 cups of milk to make just one pound of cheese!

Fried Spaghetti Cake

ACTIVE: 10 min   TOTAL: 45 min   SERVES: 2

3 cups leftover spaghetti

2 large eggs,
lightly beaten

1 cup grated part-skim
mozzarella cheese

¼ cup chopped
fresh parsley

Kosher salt and
freshly ground pepper

2 tablespoons
vegetable oil

Warm marinara sauce,
for serving

1 Combine the spaghetti, beaten eggs, mozzarella, parsley and a pinch each of salt and pepper in a large bowl and toss to combine.

2 Heat the vegetable oil in an 8-inch skillet over medium heat. Add the spaghetti mixture and press down with a spatula. Cook, until browned, about 5 minutes per side, carefully flipping the whole spaghetti cake with a spatula.

3 Slide the spaghetti cake onto a cutting board, then cut into wedges with a chef's knife. Serve with marinara sauce.

Tip

If you don't have leftover spaghetti to use for this dish, just make some! Cook 4 ounces spaghetti in salted boiling water as the label directs, then drain and let cool.

POP QUIZ

Fruit & Veggie Name Game

How well do you know your produce?
See how many of these you can name.

1 _____

2 _____

3 _____

4 _____

⑤ _____

⑥ _____

⑦ _____

⑧ _____

⑨ _____

⑩ _____

Make a three-cheese pizza! See page 112.

Dinner

Crunchy Carrot Mac and Cheese

ACTIVE: **25 min**   TOTAL: **45 min**   SERVES: **4**

- **2 tablespoons unsalted butter**
- **½ teaspoon paprika**
- **¼ teaspoon ground turmeric**
- **¼ cup panko**
- **Kosher salt**
- **2 medium carrots, halved lengthwise**
- **12 ounces elbow macaroni**
- **1½ tablespoons all-purpose flour**
- **1 teaspoon mustard powder**
- **1 12-ounce can evaporated milk**
- **1½ cups shredded American cheese**
- **1 cup shredded sharp yellow cheddar cheese**
- **Freshly ground pepper**

1 Melt 1 tablespoon butter in a medium skillet over medium heat. Add the paprika, turmeric and panko and cook, stirring with a wooden spoon, until the panko is lightly toasted, about 3 minutes; spoon into a small bowl and set aside for topping.

2 Fill a large pot with water and season with salt. Bring to a boil, then add the carrots and cook until tender, about 10 minutes. Using tongs, remove the carrots and put in a blender. Set aside.

3 Return the water in the pot to a boil. Add the macaroni and cook as the label directs for al dente. Carefully remove 1 cup of the pasta cooking water with a liquid measuring cup. Carefully drain the macaroni in a colander set in the sink. Add half of the reserved cooking water to the blender with the carrots and puree until smooth.

4 Melt the remaining 1 tablespoon butter in a medium saucepan over medium heat; whisk in the flour and mustard powder. Cook, whisking, 1 minute. Whisk in the evaporated milk and carrot puree. Simmer, whisking, until slightly thickened, about 5 minutes. Add both cheeses and whisk until melted. Add the pasta and stir to coat with a wooden spoon, adding the remaining cooking water as needed to loosen the sauce. Season with salt and pepper. Spoon into bowls and top with the panko mixture.

Did You Know?

Mac and cheese has been to space—in dehydrated form! Astronaut Mike Massimino, who went on missions in 2002 and 2009, called it the best food he ate in orbit.

Broccoli-Cheddar Soup

ACTIVE: **30 min**   TOTAL: **50 min**   SERVES: **4**

2   slices bacon, chopped

1   bunch scallions, chopped

1   stalk celery, chopped

3   tablespoons all-purpose flour

1   head broccoli, florets and tender stems chopped

2   cups low-sodium chicken broth

Kosher salt and freshly ground pepper

1   cup frozen shelled edamame, thawed

¾   cup half-and-half

1   cup shredded white cheddar cheese

1 Cook the bacon in a large Dutch oven over medium-high heat, stirring occasionally with a wooden spoon, until crisp, about 10 minutes. Remove with a slotted spoon and put on paper towels; set aside to drain.

2 Add the scallions and celery to the drippings in the pot and cook, stirring with the wooden spoon, until slightly softened, about 2 minutes. Sprinkle in the flour and cook, stirring, until incorporated. Add the broccoli, chicken broth, 3 cups water, 1 teaspoon salt and a few grinds of pepper. Increase the heat to high and bring to a boil. Add the edamame, reduce the heat to medium low and simmer until slightly thickened, about 10 minutes.

3 Working in batches, carefully ladle the soup into a blender, filling it no more than halfway. Keeping the lid slightly open at the top (cover it with a kitchen towel to prevent splatters), puree the soup until smooth. Return the soup to the pot. Stir in the half-and-half and simmer 5 minutes. Stir in the cheese and continue to cook, stirring, until the cheese melts and the soup thickens, about 5 more minutes. Season with salt and pepper. Ladle into bowls and top with the bacon.

Tip

Make sure you puree hot liquids in small batches and keep the top open a little to let steam escape. If the steam builds up, it can force the top off, causing the hot liquid to explode all over the place.

Spaghetti Marinara

ACTIVE: **20 min**   TOTAL: **40 min**   SERVES: **6**

Kosher salt

1   **pound spaghetti**

3   **tablespoons extra-virgin olive oil**

4   **cloves garlic, thinly sliced**

1   **small onion, finely chopped**

1   **teaspoon dried oregano**

1   **28-ounce can whole peeled tomatoes**

½   **cup chopped fresh basil**

2   **tablespoons unsalted butter, cut into cubes**

Tip

Before you dump your pasta cooking water, scoop out a little to use when you're finishing the dish: The starchy, salty liquid makes a nice addition to the sauce.

1 Fill a large pot with water and season with salt. Bring to a boil over high heat. Add the spaghetti and cook as the label directs for al dente. Carefully remove 1 cup of the pasta cooking water with a liquid measuring cup; set aside. Carefully drain the spaghetti in a colander set in the sink.

2 Meanwhile, heat the olive oil in a large skillet over medium heat. Add the garlic and cook until golden around the edges, about 3 minutes. Add the onion, oregano and 1 teaspoon salt. Cook, stirring with a wooden spoon, until the onion is soft but not browned, about 10 minutes. Empty the tomatoes into a bowl and crush with your hands. Add to the skillet along with ½ cup water; continue cooking until the sauce is slightly reduced, about 20 minutes. Stir in the basil and season with salt. Keep warm over low heat.

3 Add the spaghetti to the sauce along with the butter and ½ cup of the reserved cooking water. Increase the heat to medium and toss with tongs to coat, adding the remaining cooking water as needed to loosen the sauce. Use the tongs to serve the spaghetti.

Fettuccine Alfredo

ACTIVE: **20 min**   TOTAL: **30 min**   SERVES: **6**

Kosher salt

1   pound fettuccine

1½ cups heavy cream

6   tablespoons unsalted butter, cut into cubes

¼   teaspoon freshly grated nutmeg

Freshly ground pepper

1   cup grated parmesan cheese, plus more for topping

1 Fill a large pot with water and season with salt. Bring to a boil over high heat. Add the fettuccine and cook as the label directs for al dente. Carefully remove ½ cup of the pasta cooking water with a liquid measuring cup; set aside. Carefully drain the fettuccine in a colander set in the sink.

2 Meanwhile, combine the heavy cream and butter in a large skillet. Bring to a simmer over medium-high heat, whisking to combine. Whisk in the nutmeg and ½ teaspoon each salt and pepper. Keep warm over low heat.

3 Add the fettuccine and cheese to the skillet. Increase the heat to medium and toss with tongs to coat, adding the reserved cooking water as needed to loosen the sauce. Use the tongs to serve the fettuccine and top with more parmesan.

Did You Know?

There are about 600 different pasta shapes! Fettuccine is slightly wider than linguine but more narrow than tagliatelle and pappardelle.

Spaghetti with Cheeseburger Meatballs

ACTIVE: **45 min**   TOTAL: **50 min**   SERVES: **6**

Kosher salt

12 ounces spaghetti

3 stale hamburger buns

2 tablespoons extra-virgin olive oil

½ cup whole milk

1 pound ground beef

½ cup finely chopped onion

¼ cup finely chopped dill pickle slices, plus pickle slices for serving

¼ cup ketchup

1 tablespoon yellow mustard

1 tablespoon Worcestershire sauce

Freshly ground pepper

1½ ounces sharp white cheddar cheese, cut into 24 small cubes, plus grated cheese for topping

4 cloves garlic, sliced

2 tablespoons tomato paste

Thinly sliced romaine lettuce and chopped tomato, for topping

Tip
Dampen your hands with a little water before rolling your meatballs so the meat won't stick to your skin.

1 Preheat the oven to 350°. Fill a large pot with water and season with salt. Bring to a boil over high heat. Add the spaghetti and cook as the label directs for al dente. Carefully remove 1 cup of the pasta cooking water with a liquid measuring cup; set aside. Carefully drain the spaghetti in a colander set in the sink.

2 Meanwhile, put 2 hamburger buns in a food processor and pulse into coarse crumbs. Heat 1 tablespoon olive oil in a large nonstick skillet over medium heat. Add the breadcrumbs and cook, stirring, until toasted, about 3 minutes, then spoon into a bowl. Bunch up a paper towel and hold it with tongs to wipe out the skillet.

3 Tear up the remaining hamburger bun; put in a large bowl along with the milk and let soak 5 minutes. Drain, squeezing the excess milk from the bread. Return the soaked bread to the empty bowl and add half of the toasted breadcrumbs, the ground beef, onion, chopped pickles, 2 tablespoons ketchup, the mustard, Worcestershire sauce, ½ teaspoon salt and a few grinds of pepper. Mix with your hands until combined. Divide the meat mixture into 24 pieces. Press a cheese cube into the center of each and shape into meatballs around the cheese.

4 Heat the remaining 1 tablespoon olive oil in the same skillet over medium heat. Add the meatballs and cook, turning with the tongs, until browned, about 4 minutes. Arrange the meatballs on a rimmed baking sheet; place in the oven and bake until just cooked through, about 5 minutes. Reserve the skillet.

5 Add the garlic to the skillet; cook over medium heat until golden, about 30 seconds. Add the tomato paste and the remaining 2 tablespoons ketchup; cook 1 minute, then stir in the reserved pasta cooking water until smooth. Simmer until slightly thickened, about 3 minutes.

6 Add the spaghetti to the skillet and toss to coat with the tongs. Use the tongs to serve the spaghetti and top with the remaining toasted breadcrumbs, the meatballs, grated cheddar, lettuce and tomato. Serve with pickle slices.

Did You Know?

These noodles look like spaghetti but they're really spaghetti squash. The gourd got its name because its flesh can be scraped into thin pasta-like strands.

Spaghetti Squash and Meatballs

ACTIVE: **45 min**   TOTAL: **1½ hr**   SERVES: **4**

1 **medium spaghetti squash (about 2 pounds)**

Kosher salt

3 **tablespoons extra-virgin olive oil, plus more for brushing**

2 **stalks celery, chopped**

1 **medium carrot, roughly chopped**

1 **medium onion, roughly chopped**

6 **cloves garlic**

1 **cup fresh parsley**

1 **pound ground beef**

1 **pound ground pork**

2 **large eggs**

1 **cup Italian-style breadcrumbs**

1 **cup plus 3 tablespoons grated parmesan cheese**

2 **28-ounce cans tomato puree**

2 **large sprigs basil**

1 **teaspoon dried oregano**

1 Preheat the oven to 425°. Carefully cut the spaghetti squash in half lengthwise with a chef's knife and scoop out the seeds with a spoon. Sprinkle the cut sides with ½ teaspoon salt, then brush both sides with olive oil. Put the squash cut-side up in a baking dish and cover tightly with foil. Place in the oven and roast 20 minutes, then carefully remove from the oven with oven mitts and uncover. Return to the oven and continue roasting until the squash is tender, about 35 more minutes.

2 Meanwhile, make the meatballs: Brush a baking sheet with olive oil. Combine the celery, carrot, onion, garlic and parsley in a food processor and pulse to make a paste. Spoon half of the vegetable paste into a large bowl; add the ground beef, ground pork, eggs, breadcrumbs, 1 cup parmesan and 1 teaspoon salt and mix with your hands until just combined. Form into about 24 meatballs (about 2 inches each); place on the oiled baking sheet. Once the squash is done, bake the meatballs until firm but not cooked through, about 10 minutes.

3 Make the sauce: Heat 3 tablespoons olive oil in a large pot over medium-high heat. Add the remaining vegetable paste and cook, stirring occasionally with a wooden spoon, until it looks dry, about 5 minutes. Stir in the tomato puree; add 1 cup water to each empty can, then add the water to the pot (you'll get any tomato puree that's stuck to the can). Stir in the basil, oregano and 1½ teaspoons salt. Bring to a simmer, then add the meatballs and simmer until the sauce thickens and the meatballs are cooked through, 15 to 20 minutes. Remove the basil.

4 Use a fork to scrape the spaghetti squash flesh into strands; put in a large bowl and add 2 tablespoons grated parmesan. Season with salt and toss. Spoon the squash into bowls and top with the meatballs, sauce and the remaining 1 tablespoon parmesan.

Tip

This recipe makes extra meatballs and sauce. Serve them in taco shells with shredded mozzarella on top!

Rigatoni Bolognese

ACTIVE: **30 min**   TOTAL: **30 min**   SERVES: **4**

Kosher salt

12 ounces rigatoni

1 28-ounce can whole peeled tomatoes

4 cloves garlic (2 whole, 2 sliced)

Freshly ground pepper

2 tablespoons extra-virgin olive oil

1 pound ground beef

¼ cup red wine or low-sodium beef or chicken broth

1 Fill a large pot with water and season with salt. Bring to a boil over high heat. Add the rigatoni and cook as the label directs for al dente. Carefully remove ½ cup of the pasta cooking water with a liquid measuring cup; set aside. Carefully drain the rigatoni in a colander set in the sink.

2 Meanwhile, combine the tomatoes, 2 whole garlic cloves and ½ teaspoon each salt and pepper in a food processor and puree; set aside.

3 Heat the olive oil in a large saucepan over medium-high heat. Add the remaining 2 sliced garlic cloves and cook, stirring with a wooden spoon, 1 minute. Add the ground beef and cook, breaking up the meat with the wooden spoon, until browned, 5 minutes. Carefully pour out all but about 1 tablespoon of the drippings from the pan.

4 Add the wine or broth to the saucepan and cook until the pan is dry, about 3 minutes. Add the tomato puree and stir with the wooden spoon to combine. Reduce the heat to medium and simmer, stirring occasionally, until thickened, 20 minutes; season with salt and pepper.

5 Add the rigatoni to the pan and toss with the wooden spoon, adding the reserved cooking water to loosen the sauce as needed. Spoon into bowls.

Tip

This sauce is made with a little wine, but the alcohol cooks off, so there won't be any in your finished dish. If you want to skip the wine, beef or chicken broth is a good substitute.

Did You Know?

Despite the name, bolognese sauce doesn't contain the deli meat bologna. The meat sauce and lunch meat are both named after Bologna, Italy.

Cheesy Bow Ties with Roasted Broccoli and Mozzarella Skewers

ACTIVE: **30 min**   TOTAL: **40 min**   SERVES: **4**

Kosher salt

12 ounces bow tie pasta

1 small head broccoli, cut into florets

1 tablespoon extra-virgin olive oil, plus more for drizzling

3 tablespoons grated parmesan cheese

1 clove garlic, grated

2 tablespoons unsalted butter

3 tablespoons all-purpose flour

1½ cups milk

½ teaspoon dijon or yellow mustard

1½ cups shredded cheddar cheese

Freshly ground pepper

8 mini mozzarella balls (bocconcini), halved

12 cherry tomatoes, halved

1 Preheat the oven to 450°. Fill a large pot with water and season with salt. Bring to a boil over high heat. Add the pasta and cook as the label directs for al dente. Carefully drain the pasta in a colander set in the sink. Reserve the pot.

2 Meanwhile, toss the broccoli on a baking sheet with 1 tablespoon olive oil, the parmesan and garlic. Carefully place in the oven and roast until the broccoli is slightly charred and the cheese starts browning, about 12 minutes.

3 Melt the butter in the reserved pasta pot over medium heat. Sprinkle in the flour and cook, whisking, until lightly toasted, about 2 minutes. Add the milk and mustard and cook, whisking occasionally, until thick and creamy, 4 to 5 minutes. Whisk in the cheddar and season with salt and pepper; continue cooking until the cheese is melted, 1 to 2 more minutes. Stir in the pasta until coated and warmed through, about 1 minute.

4 Thread the mozzarella and tomatoes onto 8 small skewers. Drizzle with olive oil and season with salt and pepper. Serve with the pasta and broccoli.

Tip
Everything is more fun when you eat it on a stick! Try skewering your favorite veggies or fruit and cheese as an after-school snack. See page 75 for a fun idea!

Did You Know?
Bow tie pasta is also called "farfalle," the Italian word for butterflies. Which do you think these look like: bow ties or butterflies?

DESIGN YOUR OWN RECIPE

Baked Pasta

① Pick a Pasta

Preheat the oven to 450°. Fill a large pot with water and season with salt. Bring to a boil over high heat. Add 1 pound of pasta (choose from these) and cook until very al dente, 2 or 3 minutes less than the label directs. Carefully drain the pasta in a colander set in the sink.

  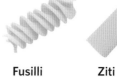 

| Bow ties | Penne | Rigatoni | Fusilli | Ziti | Large shells |

② Choose Your Mix-Ins

Pick any combination of these ingredients and combine to make 3 cups total.

Italian sausage, cooked and crumbled

Meatballs, cooked and quartered

Pepperoni, chopped

Rotisserie chicken, shredded

Roasted red peppers, sliced

Frozen artichoke hearts, thawed and chopped

Zucchini, sliced and sautéed

Mushrooms, sliced and sautéed

Eggplant, chopped and sautéed

Spinach, chopped and sautéed

③ Make the Sauce

Heat 4 cups store-bought tomato sauce in a large skillet over medium heat. Stir in one of the following ingredients, then add your meat and/or vegetable mix-ins.

 For an herb sauce: 1 cup each chopped basil and parsley

 For a creamy sauce: 1 cup fresh ricotta

For a meat sauce: ¾ pound pancetta, diced and browned

④ Prepare Your Cheese

Prep 3 cups total of melting cheese and 1 cup total of grating cheese.

MELTING CHEESES
Fresh mozzarella, cubed
Mild provolone, shredded
Italian fontina, shredded

GRATING CHEESES
Parmesan, grated
Pecorino, grated
Ricotta salata, grated

⑤ Bake the Casserole

Toss the cooked pasta with the sauce, 1½ cups of the melting cheese and ½ cup of the grating cheese. Spread in an oiled 3- to 4-quart baking dish. Sprinkle the remaining melting and grating cheeses over the top. Bake until browned, about 15 minutes. Let rest 15 minutes before serving.

Chicken Taco Cups

ACTIVE: **30 min**   TOTAL: **40 min**   SERVES: **4**

Cooking spray

4   **large flour tortillas**

3   **tablespoons all-purpose flour**

½   **teaspoon ground cumin**

½   **teaspoon chili powder**

Kosher salt and freshly ground pepper

1   **pound skinless, boneless chicken breasts, chopped**

2   **tablespoons extra-virgin olive oil**

½   **small onion, finely chopped**

2   **stalks celery, finely chopped**

2   **carrots, finely chopped**

1   **red bell pepper, finely chopped**

1   **14.5-ounce can diced fire-roasted tomatoes**

1   **cup low-sodium chicken broth**

¼   **cup chopped fresh cilantro**

1   **cup shredded monterey jack or pepper jack cheese**

1 Preheat the oven to 350˚. Coat 4 cups of a muffin pan with cooking spray. Fold each tortilla in half, then form into a cone, overlapping the sides. Fold up the point of each cone slightly, then press the tortillas into the prepared muffin pan to form a cup shape. Coat the tortillas with cooking spray. Bake until golden and crisp, about 15 minutes.

2 Meanwhile, combine the flour, cumin, chili powder, ½ teaspoon salt and a few grinds of pepper in a large bowl. Add the chicken and toss to coat.

3 Heat the olive oil in a large nonstick skillet over medium-high heat. Add the chicken in a single layer and cook, stirring occasionally with a wooden spoon, until lightly browned, about 2 minutes. Add the onion, celery, carrots and bell pepper and cook until the vegetables begin softening, about 2 minutes. Add the tomatoes and chicken broth to the skillet and bring to a simmer. Cook until the vegetables are tender and the sauce thickens slightly, about 5 minutes. Stir in the cilantro and season with salt and pepper.

4 Spoon the chicken mixture into the tortilla cups. Top with the cheese.

Did You Know?
A double "L" in Spanish is usually pronounced with a "y" sound in Mexico, which is why we say tor-tee-yah and not tor-til-lah!

Tip
Chopping raw meat is easier when the meat is slightly frozen. Pop your chicken in the freezer for about 10 minutes before you chop it.

Pepperoni Pizza Chicken Fingers

ACTIVE: **20 min**   TOTAL: **40 min**   SERVES: **4**

FOR THE CHICKEN FINGERS

- ½   cup sliced pepperoni
- ½   teaspoon Italian seasoning
- ¾   cup breadcrumbs
- 1   tablespoon extra-virgin olive oil
- 2   large eggs

Kosher salt

Cooking spray

- 2   large skinless, boneless chicken breasts, each cut into 8 strips

FOR THE DIPPING SAUCE

- 1   cup marinara sauce
- ¼   cup shredded mozzarella cheese

1 Make the chicken fingers: Preheat the oven to 425°. Pulse the pepperoni in a food processor until finely chopped. Spoon into a shallow dish and add the Italian seasoning, breadcrumbs and olive oil; stir together. Combine the eggs and a pinch of salt in a separate shallow dish and whisk until smooth.

2 Put a wire rack on a baking sheet and coat the rack with cooking spray. Dip the chicken in the egg mixture, letting any excess drip off, then coat with the pepperoni breadcrumbs, pressing firmly so they stick. Place the chicken on the prepared rack and coat generously with cooking spray. Bake until cooked through and golden brown, 15 to 20 minutes.

3 Meanwhile, make the dipping sauce: Combine the marinara sauce and mozzarella in a microwave-safe bowl. Just before serving, microwave, stirring every 30 seconds, until the sauce is hot and the cheese melts. Serve with the chicken fingers.

Tip

Use your right hand to dip the chicken in the egg mixture, then switch to your left hand to dip it in the crumbs. Otherwise you'll have a clumpy mess on your hands!

Did You Know?

Every chicken has two tenders—little strips of meat that are attached to the underside of each breast. You can make your own tenders by cutting the breast meat into strips.

Coconut Chicken Fingers

ACTIVE: **30 min**   TOTAL: **1 hr**   SERVES: **4**

FOR THE CHICKEN FINGERS

- ½ cup sweetened shredded coconut
- 1¼ cups panko
- 1 teaspoon paprika
- 3 tablespoons coconut oil, melted
- 2 large eggs
- Kosher salt
- Cooking spray
- 2 large skinless, boneless chicken breasts, each cut into 8 strips

FOR THE DIPPING SAUCE

- ⅓ cup Thai sweet chili sauce
- 2 tablespoons mayonnaise
- Juice of ½ lime

1 Make the chicken fingers: Preheat the oven to 425°. Spread the coconut on a baking sheet and bake, stirring occasionally with a spatula, until golden brown, about 10 minutes. Carefully remove the baking sheet from the oven with oven mitts and spoon the toasted coconut into a shallow dish. Let cool, then stir in the panko, paprika and coconut oil. (The mixture should look like wet sand.) Combine the eggs and ½ teaspoon salt in a separate shallow dish and whisk until smooth.

2 Put a wire rack on a baking sheet and coat the rack with cooking spray. Dip the chicken in the egg mixture, letting any excess drip off, then coat with the coconut mixture, pressing firmly so it sticks. Place the chicken on the rack and coat generously with more cooking spray. Bake until cooked through and golden brown, 15 to 20 minutes.

3 Meanwhile, make the dipping sauce: Combine the sweet chili sauce, mayonnaise and lime juice in a bowl and whisk to combine. Serve with the chicken fingers.

Hawaiian Chicken Kebabs

ACTIVE: **25 min**   TOTAL: **30 min**   SERVES: **4**

1   tablespoon vegetable oil, plus more for brushing

¾   cup ketchup

3   tablespoons soy sauce or teriyaki sauce

3   tablespoons apple cider vinegar

1½ tablespoons honey

1¼ pounds skinless, boneless chicken breasts, cut into 1¼-inch pieces

1   8-ounce can water chestnuts, drained and rinsed (optional)

4   cups chopped pineapple

1   small red or orange bell pepper, cut into chunks

Kosher salt and freshly ground pepper

4   small Hawaiian sweet rolls

1 Preheat the broiler. Line a baking sheet with foil and brush lightly with vegetable oil.

2 Meanwhile, combine the ketchup, soy sauce, vinegar and honey in a medium bowl and whisk to combine. Spoon half of the sauce into a separate bowl and set aside for dipping.

3 Combine the chicken, water chestnuts, pineapple, bell pepper and 1 tablespoon vegetable oil in a large bowl; sprinkle with ½ teaspoon salt and a few grinds of pepper and toss. Thread the chicken and vegetables onto 8 skewers, alternating the ingredients. Arrange the kebabs on the oiled baking sheet.

4 Brush the kebabs with some of the sauce and broil until the chicken and vegetables start browning, about 4 minutes. Flip the kebabs, brush with more sauce and continue broiling until the chicken is golden and cooked through, about 3 more minutes. Serve with the reserved sauce and rolls.

Did You Know?

Many people think all pineapples come from Hawaii, but the state actually produces less than 1 percent of the world's supply! Most come from Costa Rica.

Tip

If you're using wooden skewers in the oven or on the grill, soak them in water for about 20 minutes first. This keeps the skewers from burning.

Did You Know?

McDonald's sells about 75 hamburgers every second. That's more than 2 billion burgers a year!

Italian Burgers
with Spaghetti Fries

ACTIVE: **45 min**   TOTAL: **45 min**   SERVES: **4**

FOR THE FRIES

Vegetable oil, for frying
    and brushing

Kosher salt

4   ounces spaghetti

¼   cup grated
    parmesan cheese

FOR THE BURGERS

½   small onion,
    cut into chunks

4   cloves garlic, smashed

½   cup fresh basil, plus
    thinly sliced basil
    for topping

¼   cup fresh parsley

1¼   pounds ground beef

¾   cup grated
    parmesan cheese

1   cup tomato sauce,
    plus more for dipping

1   teaspoon dried oregano

Kosher salt and freshly
    ground pepper

4   slices
    mozzarella cheese

4   hamburger buns

1   tablespoon extra-virgin
    olive oil

1   Make the fries: Brush a baking sheet with vegetable oil. Carefully heat 2 to 3 inches vegetable oil in a Dutch oven until a deep-fry thermometer registers 365°. Meanwhile, bring a medium pot of salted water to a boil. Add the pasta to the boiling water and cook as the label directs, then drain. Spread the pasta in an even layer on the oiled baking sheet and let cool.

2   Cut the cooked spaghetti into short pieces with kitchen shears. Carefully add to the hot oil in batches and fry, turning once with tongs, until golden, 30 seconds to 1 minute. Remove with tongs and put on a paper towels; set aside to drain. Sprinkle with salt and the parmesan.

3   Make the burgers: Preheat the broiler. Pulse the onion, garlic, basil and parsley in a food processor until finely chopped. Scrape into a bowl and add the ground beef, ½ cup each parmesan and tomato sauce, the oregano, ½ teaspoon salt and a few grinds of pepper. Mix with your hands until combined, then form into four 1-inch-thick patties. Place on a rimmed baking sheet.

4   Carefully place the baking sheet under the broiler and broil the patties, carefully flipping with a spatula, until browned and just cooked through, 3 to 4 minutes per side. Top each patty with a slice of mozzarella and 2 tablespoons of the remaining tomato sauce. Return to the broiler until the cheese melts, about 30 seconds.

5   Place the buns split-side up on another baking sheet and toast under the broiler until just golden, 1 to 2 minutes. Brush the toasted sides lightly with the olive oil and sprinkle with the remaining ¼ cup parmesan. Return to the broiler until the cheese melts, about 30 seconds.

6   Place each patty on a bun bottom and top with some sliced basil and a bun top. Serve with the spaghetti fries and warm tomato sauce for dipping.

Tip

Be sure to have a grown-up help you make the spaghetti fries— the oil will be very hot!

Chinese Meatball Sliders with Pineapple Salad

ACTIVE: **30 min**   TOTAL: **30 min**   SERVES: **4**

Cooking spray

2   tablespoons hoisin sauce

2   tablespoons plus 1 teaspoon rice vinegar (not seasoned)

12   ounces ground pork

2   tablespoons panko

1   scallion (white and light green parts only), sliced

1   teaspoon grated peeled ginger

Kosher salt and freshly ground pepper

¼   small head green cabbage, chopped

2   small carrots, chopped

½   cup chopped pineapple

1   tablespoon mayonnaise, plus more for the buns

12   mini potato slider buns

Shredded romaine lettuce, for topping

1   Position a rack in the upper third of the oven and preheat to 425°. Coat a rimmed baking sheet with cooking spray. Combine 1 tablespoon hoisin sauce and 1 teaspoon rice vinegar in a small bowl; set aside.

2   Combine the pork, panko, the remaining 1 tablespoon hoisin sauce, the scallion, ginger, ½ teaspoon salt and a few grinds of pepper in a medium bowl. Mix with your hands until combined, then roll the mixture into twelve 1½-inch meatballs; put on the prepared baking sheet. Bake until browned, 5 to 6 minutes, then carefully remove from the oven with oven mitts and turn the meatballs with tongs. Return to the oven and bake until browned and cooked through, 5 to 6 more minutes. Remove from the oven and brush with the reserved hoisin sauce mixture.

3   Meanwhile, combine the cabbage, carrots, pineapple, the remaining 2 tablespoons rice vinegar, the mayonnaise and ½ teaspoon salt in a food processor and pulse until the vegetables and pineapple are roughly chopped.

4   Spread mayonnaise on the bottom half of each bun, then fill with some shredded lettuce and a meatball. Serve with the pineapple salad.

Tip

These meatballs get a kick from fresh ginger. To peel the knobby-looking root, scrape off the thin brown skin with the tip of a spoon.

Did You Know?

The world's largest meatball weighed a whopping 1,707.5 pounds! It was created in 2017 in South Carolina. Most of the meatball went to feed the hungry.

Sloppy Joe Fries

ACTIVE: **35 min**   TOTAL: **40 min**   SERVES: **4**

3 **large russet potatoes**

3 **tablespoons extra-virgin olive oil**

1 **teaspoon chili powder**

1 **pound ground beef**

1 **bunch scallions, sliced (white and green parts separated)**

1 **clove garlic, chopped**

¾ **cup ketchup**

2 **tablespoons packed light brown sugar**

2½ **teaspoons Worcestershire sauce**

1 **cup shredded cheddar cheese**

1 **cup cubed mozzarella**

Chopped cherry tomatoes and pickled jalapeños, for topping (optional)

1 Make the fries: Preheat the oven to 425°. Cut the potatoes into thin wedges; toss with 1 tablespoon olive oil and ½ teaspoon chili powder on a baking sheet. Spread in a single layer and bake, 15 minutes. Carefully remove from the oven with oven mitts and flip the potatoes with a spatula. Return to the oven and bake until golden, about 15 more minutes.

2 Meanwhile, heat the remaining 2 tablespoons olive oil in a large skillet over medium-high heat. Add the beef and the remaining ½ teaspoon chili powder. Cook, breaking up the meat with a wooden spoon, until browned, about 5 minutes. Add the scallion whites and garlic and cook until slightly softened, about 2 minutes. Add the ketchup, brown sugar, Worcestershire sauce and 1½ cups water; reduce the heat to medium and simmer until thickened slightly, about 8 minutes.

3 Divide the fries among plates. Top with the beef mixture, cheddar, mozzarella, scallion greens, tomatoes and pickled jalapeños.

Tip

For a speedier dinner, skip step 1 and serve the beef mixture over baked frozen fries instead.

Did You Know?

The origin of the sloppy joe sandwich is a mystery: Some say it was invented by an Iowa cook named Joe, some claim it came from Sloppy Joe's Bar in Florida, and others insist it was invented at Sloppy Joe's saloon in Havana, Cuba.

Pizza Dogs

ACTIVE: **20 min**   TOTAL: **20 min**   MAKES: **4**

- 1   **24-ounce jar marinara sauce**
- 4   **hot dogs**
- 4   **hot dog buns**

Shredded mozzarella cheese, grated parmesan cheese and dried oregano, for sprinkling

1 Preheat the broiler. Bring the marinara sauce to a simmer in a medium skillet over medium heat. Add the hot dogs and cook until warmed through, about 5 minutes.

2 Meanwhile, place the hot dog buns on a baking sheet, opening each one slightly. Broil until lightly toasted, about 2 minutes.

3 Carefully remove the baking sheet from the broiler using oven mitts. Spoon some of the marinara sauce onto each bun and put a hot dog in each with tongs. Sprinkle with mozzarella, parmesan and dried oregano. Carefully return to the broiler and broil until the cheese melts, 1 to 2 more minutes.

Cuban Dogs

ACTIVE: **25 min**   TOTAL: **25 min**   MAKES: **4**

- 1   **tablespoon unsalted butter**
- 4   **hot dogs**
- 4   **small sub rolls, split open**
- 8   **thin slices deli ham**
- 1   **dill pickle, thinly sliced lengthwise into 8 pieces**

Yellow mustard, for topping
- 8   **thin slices Swiss cheese**

Cooking spray

1 Melt the butter in a large cast-iron skillet over medium heat. Add the hot dogs and cook, turning with tongs, until warmed through, about 5 minutes. Remove the hot dogs with the tongs and put on a cutting board. Carefully cut each in half lengthwise, then crosswise with a sharp knife.

2 Put 4 hot dog pieces on the bottom of each sub roll and top each with 2 ham slices, 2 dill pickle slices, some yellow mustard and 2 Swiss cheese slices.

3 Preheat a panini press and coat with cooking spray. Add 1 sandwich, close the panini press and cook until toasted and the cheese melts. Repeat with the remaining sandwiches. (You can also cook these in a hot buttered skillet and top with another skillet flat-side down to press them down.)

Taco Dogs

ACTIVE: **20 min** TOTAL: **20 min** MAKES: **4**

Vegetable oil, for the grill pan

4 **hot dogs**

4 **small flour tortillas**

Shredded cheddar cheese, shredded lettuce, sour cream and salsa, for topping

1 Heat a grill pan over medium heat and brush the pan with vegetable oil. Carefully cut the hot dogs in half lengthwise with a sharp knife. Add the hot dogs to the grill pan and cook, turning with tongs, until marked on both sides, about 5 minutes. Remove from the pan using tongs. Add the tortillas to the pan, one at a time, and grill until toasted.

2 Put 2 hot dog halves on each tortilla. Top with cheddar, lettuce, sour cream and salsa.

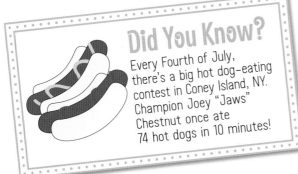

Did You Know?

Every Fourth of July, there's a big hot dog-eating contest in Coney Island, NY. Champion Joey "Jaws" Chestnut once ate 74 hot dogs in 10 minutes!

Sausage-and-Pepper Dogs

ACTIVE: **20 min** TOTAL: **20 min** MAKES: **4**

4 **hot dogs**

2 **tablespoons extra-virgin olive oil**

2 **bell peppers (any color), sliced**

1 **onion, sliced**

1 **clove garlic, finely chopped**

Pinch of cayenne pepper

Pinch of fennel seeds

4 **hoagie rolls, split open**

1 Carefully cut the hot dogs in half lengthwise with a sharp knife. Heat the olive oil in a medium skillet over medium heat. Add the hot dogs, bell peppers and onion and cook, stirring with a wooden spoon, until the hot dogs are warmed through and the vegetables are tender, 5 to 7 minutes. Add the garlic, cayenne, fennel seeds and a splash of water and stir to combine.

2 Meanwhile, toast the hoagie rolls in a toaster oven. Using tongs, pile the hot dogs, peppers and onion on the hoagie rolls.

Did You Know?

Americans eat about 4.5 billion tacos a year. That's 490,000 miles of tacos—enough to make it to the moon and back!

Sausage-Pepperoni Pizza Tacos

ACTIVE: **30 min**   TOTAL: **30 min**   SERVES: **4**

2 tablespoons extra-virgin olive oil

4 ounces white mushrooms, thinly sliced

8 ounces sweet Italian sausage (preferably without fennel seeds), casings removed

2 ounces sliced pepperoni, halved (about ½ cup)

¼ teaspoon dried oregano

1 cup pizza sauce

8 corn tortillas

1 cup shredded mozzarella cheese

½ cup ricotta cheese

Thinly sliced fresh basil, for topping

1 Heat 1 tablespoon olive oil in a large skillet over medium-high heat. Add the mushrooms and cook, without stirring, until browned, then stir with a wooden spoon and continue to cook until browned all over, about 3 minutes. Remove to a plate.

2 Reduce the heat to medium and add the remaining 1 tablespoon olive oil to the skillet. Add the sausage and cook, breaking it up with the wooden spoon, until browned, 3 to 5 minutes. Add the pepperoni and oregano and cook until the pepperoni is crisp around the edges, about 1 minute. Stir in the pizza sauce and reserved mushrooms. Bring to a simmer and cook 5 more minutes.

3 Spoon the sausage mixture onto the tortillas. Top with the mozzarella, ricotta and basil.

Tip
To warm up your tortillas, toast them one at a time in a dry skillet until just golden, or wrap a stack in a damp paper towel and microwave for a few seconds.

Three-Cheese Bacon Pizza

ACTIVE: **25 min**   TOTAL: **40 min**   SERVES: **4 (makes 2 pies)**

1   pound store-bought
    pizza dough, at
    room temperature

All-purpose flour,
    for dusting

4   slices bacon, chopped

1   8-ounce can
    tomato sauce

2   tablespoons
    extra-virgin olive oil

1   clove garlic, grated

¼   teaspoon dried oregano

Kosher salt and freshly
    ground pepper

1   cup shredded
    mozzarella cheese

1   cup shredded white
    cheddar cheese

1   tablespoon grated
    parmesan cheese

1 Place a pizza stone or upside-down baking sheet on the bottom rack of the oven and preheat to 475°. Roll out the pizza dough on a floured surface with a rolling pin into a 9-inch round. Lightly dust a parchment-covered pizza peel with flour (or use another upside-down baking sheet). Put the dough on the parchment. Carefully slide the pizza and parchment onto the hot stone and bake until the crust is lightly golden and puffy, about 7 minutes.

2 Meanwhile, cook the bacon in a large skillet over medium heat, stirring with a wooden spoon, until crisp, about 6 minutes. Spoon the bacon onto paper towels and let drain. Combine the tomato sauce, olive oil, garlic and oregano in a medium bowl; season with salt and pepper.

3 Carefully slide the crust and parchment back onto the pizza peel or upside-down baking sheet and remove from the oven. Let cool slightly, then carefully slice the crust in half horizontally with a serrated knife to make 2 thin crusts.

4 Turn the pizza crusts cut-side up on the parchment-lined pizza peel. Spread the sauce mixture over the crusts, then sprinkle with the mozzarella, cheddar and bacon. Slide the pizzas and parchment back onto the hot stone and bake until the cheese melts and the crust is golden, about 8 more minutes. Sprinkle with the parmesan.

Tip

After your pizzas come out of the oven, give them a few minutes before you slice them. This will let the cheese cool a little so it doesn't ooze all over the place.

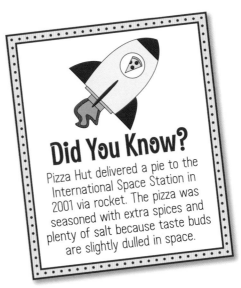

Did You Know?

Pizza Hut delivered a pie to the International Space Station in 2001 via rocket. The pizza was seasoned with extra spices and plenty of salt because taste buds are slightly dulled in space.

Tex-Mex Pizza

ACTIVE: **25 min**   TOTAL: **30 min**   SERVES: **4 to 6**

1 **pound store-bought pizza dough, at room temperature**

All-purpose flour, for dusting

Extra-virgin olive oil, for brushing

¾ **cup canned refried black beans**

½ **cup salsa**

1½ **cups grated sharp cheddar cheese**

3 **scallions, finely chopped**

¼ **cup sliced pickled jalapeños**

¼ **cup sour cream**

Juice of 1 lime

½ **cup sliced romaine lettuce**

½ **tomato, chopped**

Kosher salt

Fresh cilantro, for topping

1 Place a pizza stone or upside-down baking sheet on the bottom rack of the oven and preheat to 450°. Roll out the pizza dough on a lightly floured surface with a rolling pin into an 11-inch round. Put the dough on a parchment-covered pizza peel (or use another upside-down baking sheet). Brush the dough with olive oil, then spread the refried beans on top, leaving a ½-inch border around the edge. Spoon the salsa over the beans and sprinkle with the cheese. Scatter the scallions and jalapeños on top. Carefully slide the pizza and parchment onto the hot stone and bake until the crust is crisp, 8 to 10 minutes. Carefully slide the pizza and parchment back onto the pizza peel or upside-down baking sheet and slide onto a cutting board. Let cool a few minutes.

2 Meanwhile, combine the sour cream, half of the lime juice and 1 tablespoon water in a small bowl. In another bowl, toss the lettuce, tomato and the remaining lime juice in a separate bowl; season with salt.

3 Top the pizza with the salad, then drizzle with the sour cream mixture and sprinkle with cilantro. Cut into slices.

Tip

A pizza stone is a large piece of stone that goes in your oven. It gets super hot, so when you bake your pizza on it, the crust ends up extra crispy. If you don't have a stone, just use an upside-down baking sheet.

Did You Know?

Pizza is the most popular food on Instagram. Users post an average of 190,000 #pizza posts every day!

Turkey Meatloaf TV Dinner

ACTIVE: **20 min**   TOTAL: **1 hr 10 min**   SERVES: **4**

FOR THE MEATLOAF

Cooking spray

1¼ pounds ground turkey

1 small onion, grated

⅓ cup breadcrumbs

1 stalk celery,
   finely chopped

1 large egg, lightly beaten

½ cup ketchup

1 tablespoon chopped
   fresh parsley

Kosher salt and freshly
   ground pepper

2 teaspoons soy sauce

1 teaspoon
   Worcestershire sauce

FOR THE SIDES

1½ pounds russet potatoes,
   peeled and quartered

Kosher salt

3 tablespoons unsalted
   butter, at room
   temperature

½ cup 2% milk, warmed

Freshly ground pepper

1½ cups frozen peas

1 Make the meatloaf: Preheat the oven to 375°. Coat a 9-by-5-inch loaf pan with cooking spray. Put the turkey, onion, breadcrumbs, celery, egg, 2 tablespoons ketchup, the parsley, ½ teaspoon salt and a few grinds of pepper in a bowl. Mix with your hands until just combined, then scrape into the loaf pan.

2 Combine the remaining ¼ cup plus 2 tablespoons ketchup with the soy sauce and Worcestershire sauce in a small bowl; spread 2 tablespoons of the ketchup mixture over the meatloaf with a rubber spatula. Carefully place in the oven and bake until the top begins to brown, about 30 minutes. Carefully remove from the oven using oven mitts. Spread the remaining ketchup mixture over the meatloaf, return to the oven and continue baking until browned and a thermometer inserted into the center registers 165°, 15 to 20 more minutes. Carefully remove from the oven and let stand 5 minutes, then remove to a cutting board with a spatula and slice.

3 Meanwhile, make the mashed potatoes: Put the potatoes in a large saucepan and cover with cold water; season with salt. Bring to a simmer and cook over medium-low heat until tender, about 30 minutes. Carefully drain the potatoes in a colander set in the sink, then return to the saucepan and add the butter. Mash with a potato masher, then add the warm milk and season with salt and pepper; continue mashing until fluffy.

4 Put the peas in a microwave-safe bowl, sprinkle with water and season with salt and pepper. Cover and microwave until warmed through, about 4 minutes. Serve the meatloaf with the peas and mashed potatoes.

Tip

When making meatloaf, meatballs or burgers, try your best not to handle the ground meat too much. Overworking the meat makes it tough.

Did You Know?

The first TV dinner came out in 1954 and cost 98 cents. It was modeled after a Thanksgiving feast and contained turkey, gravy, stuffing, sweet potatoes and peas.

What's Your Hot Dog IQ?

See how well you know your franks.

1 **The length of a standard hot dog is:**

A. 6 inches **B.** 10 inches

C. 9 inches **D.** 12 inches

2 **When is peak hot dog season?**

A. Winter **B.** Spring

C. Summer **D.** Fall

3 **How did the hot dog likely get its name?**

A. Early vendors (mainly German immigrants) originally called hot dogs "dachshund sausages."

B. Hot spices were common in original hot dog recipes.

C. The creator of the hot dog was German immigrant Charles Dachshund.

D. The classic method of cooking sausages in boiling water led to the name.

4 America's favorite hot dog topping is:

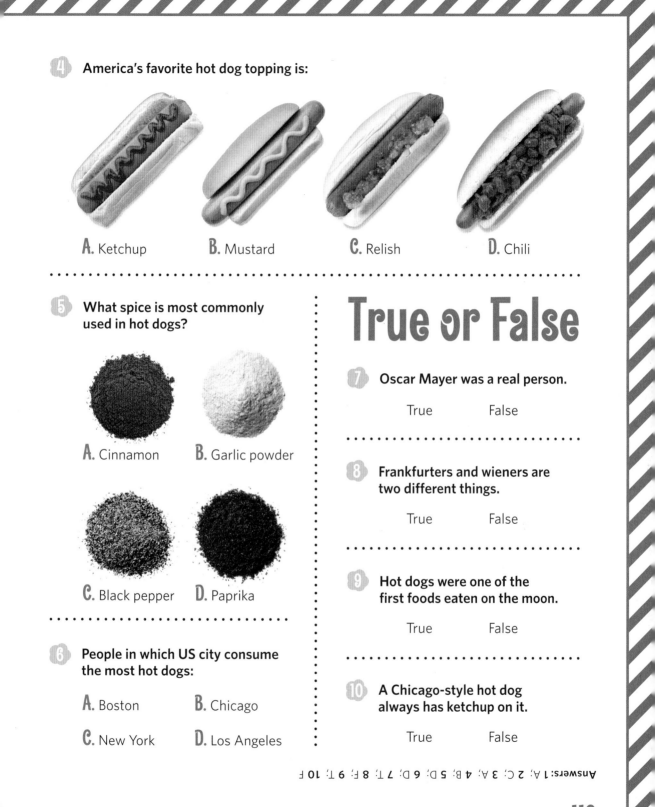

A. Ketchup   **B.** Mustard   **C.** Relish   **D.** Chili

5 What spice is most commonly used in hot dogs?

A. Cinnamon   **B.** Garlic powder

C. Black pepper   **D.** Paprika

6 People in which US city consume the most hot dogs:

A. Boston   **B.** Chicago

C. New York   **D.** Los Angeles

True or False

7 Oscar Mayer was a real person.

    True   False

8 Frankfurters and wieners are two different things.

    True   False

9 Hot dogs were one of the first foods eaten on the moon.

    True   False

10 A Chicago-style hot dog always has ketchup on it.

    True   False

Answers: 1 A; 2 C; 3 A; 4 B; 5 D; 6 D; 7 T; 8 F; 9 T; 10 F

Make a fun twist on chocolate chip cookies! See page 144.

120

Dessert

Strawberry-Shortcake Parfait Pops

ACTIVE: 20 min   TOTAL: 20 min (plus 4 hr freezing)   MAKES: 6

Cooking spray

1½ cups Special K Red Berries cereal

½ cup unsweetened shredded coconut

¾ cup vanilla frozen yogurt, slightly softened

¾ cup strawberry sorbet, slightly softened

Tip

To soften ice cream or sorbet, leave the carton out on the counter for 10 to 15 minutes. If you overdo it in the microwave, you'll end up with ice cream soup!

1 Coat the insides of six 3-ounce paper cups with cooking spray. Combine the cereal and coconut in a food processor and pulse until coarsely ground.

2 Spoon about 1 tablespoon of the cereal mixture into the bottom of each paper cup and top each with 1 tablespoon frozen yogurt. Add 2 tablespoons sorbet to each cup and press with the back of a spoon, then pack in another 1 tablespoon frozen yogurt. Sprinkle each with more of the cereal mixture. Insert a wooden stick into the center of each pop and freeze until firm, at least 4 hours.

3 Just before serving, snip the sides of the paper cups with kitchen scissors and peel off.

Italian Ice

ACTIVE: **10 min**   TOTAL: **10 min (plus 2½ hr freezing)**   MAKES: **4 cups**

3 **cups halved strawberries or chopped pineapple**

2 **tablespoons sugar**

2 **tablespoons honey**

1 **tablespoon fresh lemon juice**

1 Combine the fruit, sugar, honey, lemon juice and 2 cups ice in a food processor or blender and pulse until chunky. Add another 1 cup ice and blend until completely smooth.

2 Pour the mixture into a shallow baking dish and freeze 30 minutes. Scrape the ice with a fork until slushy, then freeze until firm, about 2 more hours.

Did You Know?

Ice cream, gelato and sherbet each contain milk or cream, while sorbet, Italian ice and snow cones do not.

Ice Cream Sundae Cones

ACTIVE: **30 min** TOTAL: **40 min (plus 3 hr freezing)** MAKES: **6**

- **6** waffle cones
- **1** cup malted milk balls, plus 6 more for the cones
- **4** large chocolate-covered peanut butter cups
- **2** quarts vanilla and/or chocolate ice cream
- **¼** cup chocolate fudge sauce
- **1** 7-ounce bottle chocolate shell topping
- **½** cup roasted peanuts, finely chopped

1 Place a stainless-steel bowl in the freezer for 20 minutes. Meanwhile, set 6 tall glasses on a baking sheet and put a waffle cone in each (the glasses will keep the cones upright). Drop 1 malted milk ball into each cone.

2 Roughly chop the remaining malted milk balls and the peanut butter cups with a chef's knife and put in the cold bowl. Add the ice cream. Smash and stir the candies into the ice cream with a metal spoon, working quickly to keep it from melting.

3 Press 1 small scoop of the ice cream into each cone. Spoon a heaping teaspoon of fudge sauce on top, then top with 2 generous scoops of the ice cream. Freeze the cones (in the glasses) until firm, about 2 hours.

4 Pour the chocolate shell topping into a bowl. Remove the cones from the glasses and dip the ice cream in the chocolate shell, swirling to coat. Immediately sprinkle the peanuts over the chocolate and place the cones upright in the glasses. Freeze until the chocolate shell is set, at least 1 hour or overnight.

Tip

Keep a container of hot water handy when you're serving ice cream so you can warm up the scoop. It'll make for easier scooping!

Cherry-Peach Twin Pops

ACTIVE: 15 min   TOTAL: 15 min (plus 4 hr freezing)   MAKES: 6 to 8

1½ **cups sour-cherry juice or nectar**

3 **tablespoons superfine sugar**

1½ **cups peach nectar**

1 Combine the cherry juice and sugar in a large bowl and whisk until the sugar dissolves. Pour half of the cherry juice mixture into 3 or 4 ice pop molds, filling them to different heights. Pour half of the peach nectar into 3 or 4 more pop molds, filling them to different heights. Freeze until firm, about 2 hours.

2 Fill the cherry pops with the remaining peach nectar and fill the peach pops with the remaining cherry juice mixture. Insert wooden sticks into the pops and freeze until firm, at least 2 hours or overnight. To release the pops, run the molds under warm water.

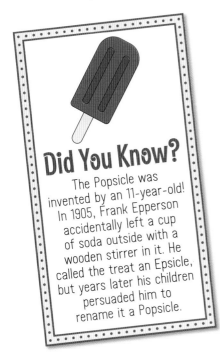

Did You Know?

The Popsicle was invented by an 11-year-old! In 1905, Frank Epperson accidentally left a cup of soda outside with a wooden stirrer in it. He called the treat an Epsicle, but years later his children persuaded him to rename it a Popsicle.

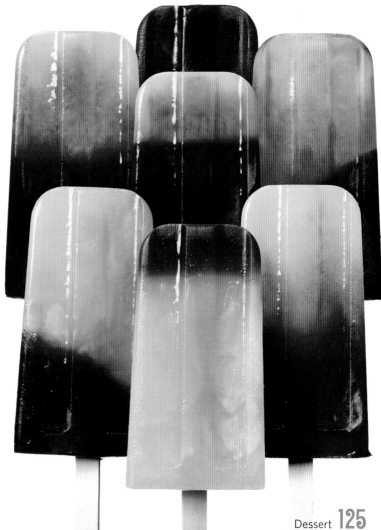

Frozen Yogurt Banana Pops

ACTIVE: **15 min**   TOTAL: **30 min (plus 3 hr freezing)**   MAKES: **8**

2   bananas

**Strawberry yogurt,
     for dipping**

**Sliced nuts, granola,
     shredded coconut,
     and/or crushed
     freeze-dried fruit,
     for sprinkling**

1 Cut the bananas in half crosswise with a chef's knife, then cut each in half lengthwise. Insert a wooden stick into the bottom of each. Put on a baking sheet and freeze until firm, about 3 hours.

2 Dip each banana in yogurt to coat and sprinkle with nuts, granola, coconut and/or freeze-dried fruit. Return to the baking sheet and freeze until set, about 10 minutes.

Tip
Freeze extra bananas in a resealable plastic bag and use them to make "nice cream." Blend the frozen bananas in a food processor with a splash of milk until it's the consistency of soft serve.

Did You Know?

The first ice cream sandwiches were sold from a pushcart in New York City in 1899 and cost two or three pennies each!

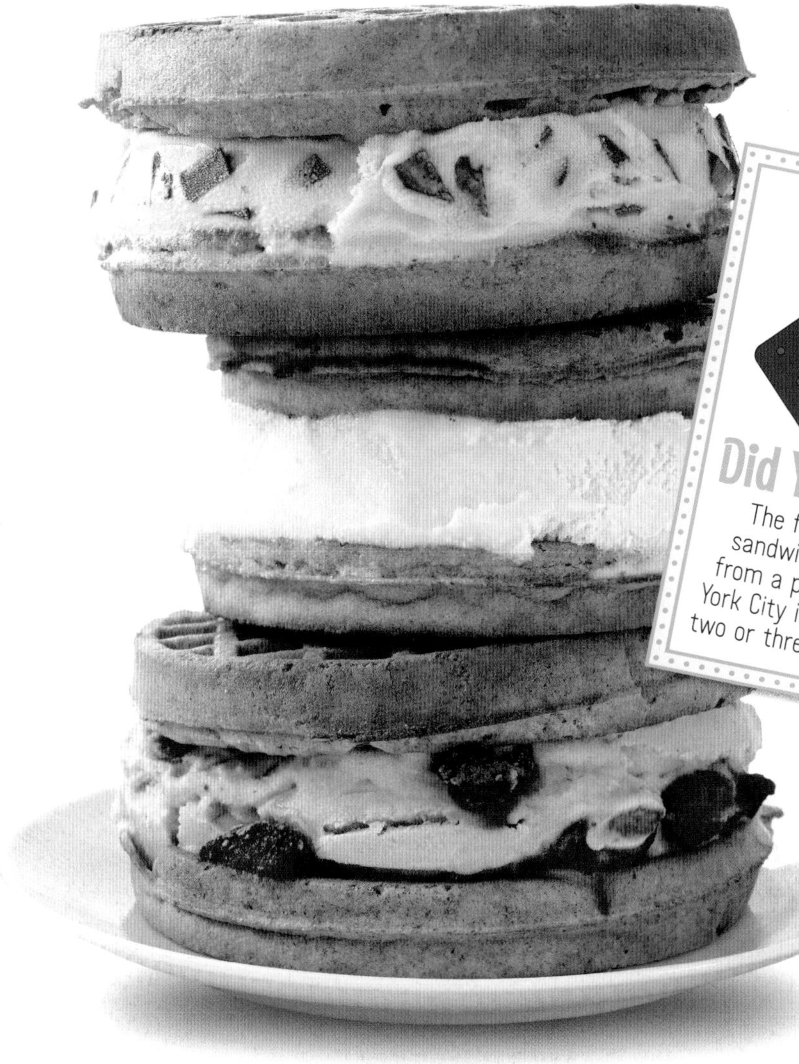

Ice Cream Wafflewich

ACTIVE: **10 min** TOTAL: **10 min** MAKES: **1**

- **2 frozen waffles**
- **2 to 3 small scoops mint chocolate chip, vanilla or cherry-vanilla ice cream**

1. Toast the waffles in a toaster until crisp. Remove and let cool completely.

2. Scoop the ice cream onto 1 waffle, then top with the other waffle, gently pressing. Keep frozen until ready to serve.

FUN WITH ICE CREAM SANDWICHES

French Toast Ice Cream Sandwich

ACTIVE: **10 min**   TOTAL: **10 min (plus 1 hr freezing)**   MAKES: **1**

Sandwich slightly softened **French vanilla ice cream** between cooled **French toast** slices. Freeze until firm, about 1 hour. Dust with **confectioners' sugar** before serving.

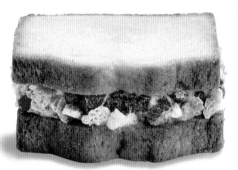

Cereal and Milk Ice Cream Sandwich

ACTIVE: **10 min**   TOTAL: **10 min (plus 1 hr freezing)**   MAKES: **1**

Sandwich slightly softened **vanilla ice cream** between **pound cake** slices; press the edges in crushed **fruity cereal.** Freeze until firm, about 1 hour.

Strawberry PB&J Ice Cream Sandwich

ACTIVE: **10 min**   TOTAL: **10 min (plus 1 hr freezing)**   MAKES: **1**

Spread **peanut butter** on sliced **sandwich bread,** then top with slightly softened **strawberry ice cream** and another slice of bread. Freeze until firm, about 1 hour. Cut into triangles.

Double Cookie Ice Cream Sandwich

ACTIVE: 10 min   TOTAL: 10 min (plus 1 hr freezing)   MAKES: 1

Sandwich slightly softened **cookie dough ice cream** between soft **chocolate chip cookies.** Freeze until firm, about 1 hour.

Banana Split Ice Cream Sandwich

ACTIVE: 10 min   TOTAL: 10 min (plus 1 hr freezing)   MAKES: 1

Sandwich slightly softened **neapolitan ice cream,** chopped **maraschino cherries** and chopped **bananas** between **banana bread** slices. Freeze until firm, about 1 hour.

Birthday Cake Ice Cream Sandwich

ACTIVE: 10 min   TOTAL: 10 min (plus 1 hr freezing)   MAKES: 1

Cut **vanilla cake** slices in half horizontally. Sandwich slightly softened **vanilla ice cream** between the cake halves. Press the sides in **rainbow nonpareils.** Top with **vanilla frosting** and more nonpareils.

ICE CREAM MASH-UP

What to Do

1 Let 1 pint vanilla ice cream soften slightly at room temperature. Scoop into a large bowl.

2 Add 2 mix-ins to the ice cream (1 to 1½ cups total). Chop anything that's large first, like brownies or cookies. Stir and mash until combined.

3 Transfer to a resealable container and freeze until firm, at least 30 minutes.

Breakfast Blast

Mix in 1 cup cinnamon cereal and ¼ cup strawberry jam.

Crazy for Caramel

Mix in 1 cup chopped caramel corn and ½ cup chopped brownies.

Say Cheesecake

Mix in ½ cup chopped cheesecake and ½ cup chopped blondies.

Snack Attack

Mix in 1 cup chopped thick-cut potato chips
and ½ cup chopped malted milk balls.

Salty-Sweet Crunch

Mix in 1 cup chopped peanut butter–filled pretzels
and ½ cup chopped semisweet chocolate.

Berry Lemonade

Mix in 1 cup chopped freeze-dried raspberries
and ½ cup lemon curd.

Smart Cookie

Mix in ½ cup blueberries
and 1 cup chopped oatmeal cookies.

Classic Vanilla Cupcakes

ACTIVE: 35 min   TOTAL: 1½ hr   MAKES: 12

FOR THE CUPCAKES

- 1⅓ cups all-purpose flour
- 1 teaspoon baking powder
- ½ teaspoon salt
- 1 stick unsalted butter, at room temperature
- 1 cup granulated sugar
- 2 large eggs
- 2 teaspoons pure vanilla extract
- ½ cup whole milk

FOR THE FROSTING

- 4 tablespoons unsalted butter, at room temperature
- 6 ounces cream cheese, at room temperature
- 1 teaspoon pure vanilla extract
- Pinch of salt
- 2 cups confectioners' sugar
- Rainbow nonpareils, for topping

1 Make the cupcakes: Preheat the oven to 350° and line a 12-cup muffin pan with paper liners. Combine the flour, baking powder and salt in a medium bowl and whisk to combine. Beat the butter in a separate large bowl with a mixer on medium-high speed until smooth, about 1 minute. Add the granulated sugar and beat until creamy, about 4 more minutes. Beat in the eggs, one at a time, then the vanilla. Beat in the flour mixture in three batches on low speed, alternating with the milk. Beat on medium-high speed until just combined.

2 Divide the batter among the muffin cups. Bake until a toothpick inserted into the centers of the cupcakes comes out clean, 20 to 25 minutes. Place the pan on a rack and let the cupcakes cool 5 minutes, then remove them to the rack to cool completely.

3 Make the frosting: Combine the butter, cream cheese, vanilla and salt in a large bowl and beat with a mixer on medium speed until creamy, 1 to 2 minutes. Slowly beat in 2 cups confectioners' sugar on medium-low speed until smooth, then beat on medium high until thick and fluffy, 1 to 2 more minutes. Frost the cupcakes and sprinkle with nonpareils.

Did You Know?

We call these itty-bitty balls nonpareils (non-puh-rells), but they're known as "hundreds and thousands" in the UK, Australia and New Zealand. They roll all over the place, so you might want to decorate on a rimmed baking sheet!

Root Beer Float Cupcakes

ACTIVE: **35 min**   TOTAL: **1½ hr**   MAKES: **12**

FOR THE CUPCAKES

- **1   cup all-purpose flour**
- **½   teaspoon baking soda**
- **½   teaspoon salt**
- **¼   cup whole milk**
- **½   cup root beer**
- **½   cup unsweetened cocoa powder**
- **1   cup granulated sugar**
- **¾   cup vegetable oil**
- **1   large egg**
- **1   teaspoon pure vanilla extract**

FOR THE FROSTING

- **1½ sticks (12 tablespoons) unsalted butter, at room temperature**
- **3   cups confectioners' sugar**
- **Pinch of salt**
- **2   teaspoons pure vanilla extract**
- **2   tablespoons root beer**
- **2   tablespoons whole milk**
- **Root beer candies, for topping**

1 Make the cupcakes: Preheat the oven to 350° and line a 12-cup muffin pan with paper liners. Combine the flour, baking soda and salt in a medium bowl and whisk to combine; set aside. Heat the milk and root beer together in a microwave-safe bowl until hot but not boiling. Put the cocoa powder in a large bowl, pour in the milk mixture and whisk until smooth; let cool slightly.

2 Add the granulated sugar, vegetable oil, egg and vanilla to the bowl with the cocoa-milk mixture and whisk until smooth. Add the flour mixture and whisk until just combined.

3 Divide the batter among the muffin cups. Bake until a toothpick inserted into the centers of the cupcakes comes out clean, 20 to 25 minutes. Place the pan on a rack and let the cupcakes cool 5 minutes, then remove them to the rack to cool completely.

4 Make the frosting: Combine the butter, confectioners' sugar and salt in a large bowl and beat with a mixer on medium speed until combined. Add the vanilla and root beer and beat on medium-high speed until creamy, about 3 minutes. Beat in the milk until fluffy, about 1 more minute. Frost the cupcakes and top with root beer candies.

Tip

Fill your cupcake liners no more than two-thirds of the way with batter. Any more than that and they could overflow in the oven!

Strawberries and Cream Cupcakes

ACTIVE: **35 min**   TOTAL: **1½ hr**   MAKES: **12**

FOR THE CUPCAKES

- **1** cup strawberries, stems removed
- **1⅓** cups all-purpose flour
- **1** teaspoon baking powder
- **½** teaspoon salt
- **1** stick unsalted butter, at room temperature
- **1** cup granulated sugar
- **2** large eggs
- **2** teaspoons pure vanilla extract
- **½** cup whole milk

FOR THE FROSTING

- **1** cup cold heavy cream
- **⅓** cup confectioners' sugar
- **1** teaspoon pure vanilla extract
- Red sprinkles, for topping
- Sliced strawberries, for topping

1 Make the cupcakes: Preheat the oven to 350° and line a 12-cup muffin pan with paper liners. Puree the strawberries in a food processor; set aside. Combine the flour, baking powder and salt in a medium bowl and whisk to combine. Beat the butter in a separate large bowl with a mixer on medium-high speed until smooth, about 1 minute. Add the granulated sugar and beat until creamy, about 4 more minutes. Beat in the eggs, one at a time, then the vanilla. Beat in the flour mixture in three batches on low speed, alternating with the milk. Beat on medium-high speed until just combined. Add ¼ cup of the strawberry puree to the batter and beat until combined.

2 Divide the batter among the muffin cups. Bake until a toothpick inserted into the centers of the cupcakes comes out clean, 20 to 25 minutes. Place the pan on a rack and let the cupcakes cool 5 minutes, then remove them to the rack to cool completely.

3 Make the frosting: Combine the heavy cream, confectioners' sugar, the remaining strawberry puree and the vanilla in a large bowl and beat with a mixer until stiff peaks form. Frost the cupcakes and top with red sprinkles and sliced strawberries.

Tip

Take your butter out of the fridge 30 minutes to 1 hour before you start baking so it softens. If you forget, just cut the butter into pieces and microwave for 5 seconds at a time until it's slightly soft.

Gluten-Free Chocolate Cupcakes

ACTIVE: **35 min**   TOTAL: **1½ hr**   MAKES: **12**

FOR THE CUPCAKES
- ⅓ **cup brown rice flour**
- ⅓ **cup sorghum flour**
- ⅓ **cup tapioca flour**
- ½ **teaspoon baking soda**
- ½ **teaspoon salt**
- ¾ **cup whole milk**
- ½ **cup unsweetened cocoa powder**
- 1 **cup granulated sugar**
- ¾ **cup vegetable oil**
- 2 **large eggs**
- 1 **teaspoon pure vanilla extract**

FOR THE FROSTING
- 4 **ounces semisweet chocolate, finely chopped**
- 1 **stick unsalted butter, at room temperature**
- 2 **cups confectioners' sugar (make sure your brand is gluten-free)**
- 2 **tablespoons unsweetened cocoa powder**
- 2 **tablespoons whole milk**
- 1 **teaspoon pure vanilla extract**

1. Make the cupcakes: Preheat the oven to 350° and line a 12-cup muffin pan with paper liners. Combine the brown rice flour, sorghum flour, tapioca flour, baking soda and salt in a medium bowl and whisk to combine. Heat the milk in a small saucepan over low heat until hot but not boiling; pour over the cocoa powder in a large bowl and whisk until smooth. Let cool slightly. Whisk in the granulated sugar, vegetable oil, eggs and vanilla until smooth. Whisk in the flour mixture until just combined.

2. Divide the batter among the muffin cups. Bake until a toothpick inserted into the centers of the cupcakes comes out clean, 20 to 25 minutes. Place the pan on a rack and let the cupcakes cool 5 minutes, then remove them to the rack to cool completely.

3. Make the frosting: Put the chocolate in a microwave-safe bowl and microwave, stirring every 30 seconds, until melted; let cool slightly. Combine the butter, confectioners' sugar, melted chocolate, cocoa powder, milk and vanilla in a food processor and pulse until smooth. Frost the cupcakes.

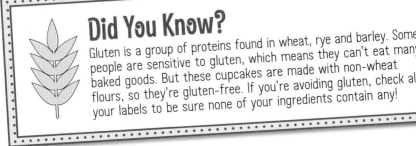

Did You Know?
Gluten is a group of proteins found in wheat, rye and barley. Some people are sensitive to gluten, which means they can't eat many baked goods. But these cupcakes are made with non-wheat flours, so they're gluten-free. If you're avoiding gluten, check all your labels to be sure none of your ingredients contain any!

Cupcakes A to Z

What to Do

1 Make Classic Vanilla Cupcakes (see page 132) and frost.

2 Pick your letters (spell out a friend's name!), then trim candies to look like the letters.

3 Arrange the candies on the cupcakes.

Gummy cherry

Sour straw

Licorice wheel

Sour twist pieces

Licorice wheel

Sour tape

Chocolate jelly ring

Gummy worm

Gummy ring

Gummy pink grapefruit wedge

Gummy strawberries

Gummy ring

Gummy fruit slice

Chocolate pretzel

Wafer cookie

Gummy cola bottle

Mini candy cane

Chuckles jelly candy

Sour tape

Licorice wheel

Gummy worms

Banana runts

Circus peanuts

Candy blocks

Swedish fish

Candy necklace
(Remove the string!)

Coconut Cereal-Treat Carrots

ACTIVE: **35 min**   TOTAL: **1 hr 35 min**   MAKES: **12**

- **3 tablespoons unsalted butter, plus more for the pan**
- **4 cups marshmallows (about 7 ounces)**
- **Orange gel food coloring**
- **4 cups crisp rice cereal**
- **1 cup sweetened shredded coconut**
- **Green sour apple twists or licorice twists, for topping**

1 Line a 9-inch pie plate with plastic wrap, leaving an overhang. Lightly butter the plastic wrap and set the pan aside.

2 Melt the butter in a medium saucepan over low heat. Add the marshmallows and stir with a wooden spoon until melted and smooth, about 3 minutes. Tint bright orange with a few drops of food coloring. Take the pan off the heat and stir in the cereal and coconut until well coated.

3 Scrape the mixture into the pie plate with a rubber spatula. Fold the overhanging plastic wrap over the mixture and press to evenly pack it into the dish. Let cool until firm, about 1 hour.

4 Meanwhile, cut the sour apple twists into 3-inch pieces with kitchen scissors. Use the scissors to fringe the candy, leaving about ½ inch connected at one end.

5 Lift the cereal treats out of the pan and place upside down on a cutting board; peel off the plastic wrap. Cut into 12 wedges with a chef's knife. Make a hole in the rounded edge of each wedge with a skewer and press in the candy to look like a carrot top.

Tip
Gel food coloring is much more concentrated than the liquid stuff, so you can use less of it and still get a super-bright color. It's great for dyeing cake batter, too.

Did You Know?
Snap, Crackle and Pop have been the cartoon mascots of Rice Krispies cereal since 1933. They were originally drawn as older gnomes, but they were later redesigned to look younger.

SNAP! CRACKLE! POP!

Triple Chocolate Mug Cakes

ACTIVE: **10 min**   TOTAL: **25 min**   MAKES: **4**

**Unsalted butter,
for the mugs**

½   **cup sugar**

½   **cup buttermilk**

¼   **cup vegetable oil**

1   **large egg**

½   **teaspoon pure
vanilla extract**

⅓   **cup all-purpose flour**

2   **tablespoons Dutch-
process cocoa powder**

⅛   **teaspoon baking soda**

Pinch of salt

**Chocolate ice cream and
chocolate sprinkles,
for topping**

1 Lightly butter 4 small microwave-safe mugs. Combine the sugar, buttermilk, vegetable oil, egg and vanilla in a large bowl and whisk until smooth, about 2 minutes. Whisk in the flour, cocoa powder, baking soda and salt until just combined.

2 Spoon about ⅓ cup of the batter into each mug. Microwave 1 mug until puffed and a toothpick inserted into the center comes out clean, about 2 minutes. (Continue microwaving 15 seconds at a time, if needed.) Repeat with the remaining mugs, microwaving one at a time. Let cool slightly. Top with small scoops of chocolate ice cream and chocolate sprinkles.

Tip

To make vanilla mug cakes, use ½ cup flour instead of ⅓ cup and leave out the cocoa powder. Top with whipped cream and rainbow sprinkles.

Gluten-Free Blueberry Cheesecake Mug Cakes

ACTIVE: 10 min   TOTAL: 25 min   MAKES: 4

Unsalted butter,
   for the mugs

8   ounces cream cheese

1   large egg

¼   cup confectioners'
   sugar (make sure your
   brand is gluten-free)

2   tablespoons cornstarch

1   teaspoon fresh
   lemon juice

1   teaspoon pure
   vanilla extract

Pinch of salt

4   teaspoons
   dried blueberries

Blueberry preserves,
   for topping

1 Lightly butter 4 small microwave-safe mugs. Microwave the cream cheese in a large microwave-safe bowl until soft, about 30 seconds. Add the egg, confectioners' sugar, cornstarch, lemon juice, vanilla and salt and whisk until smooth.

2 Spoon about ¼ cup of the batter into each mug, then stir 1 teaspoon dried blueberries into each. Microwave 1 mug until puffed and a toothpick inserted into the center comes out clean, about 2 minutes. (Continue microwaving 15 seconds at a time, if needed.) Repeat with the remaining mugs, microwaving one at a time. Let cool slightly. Top with blueberry preserves.

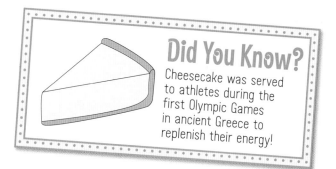

Did You Know?

Cheesecake was served to athletes during the first Olympic Games in ancient Greece to replenish their energy!

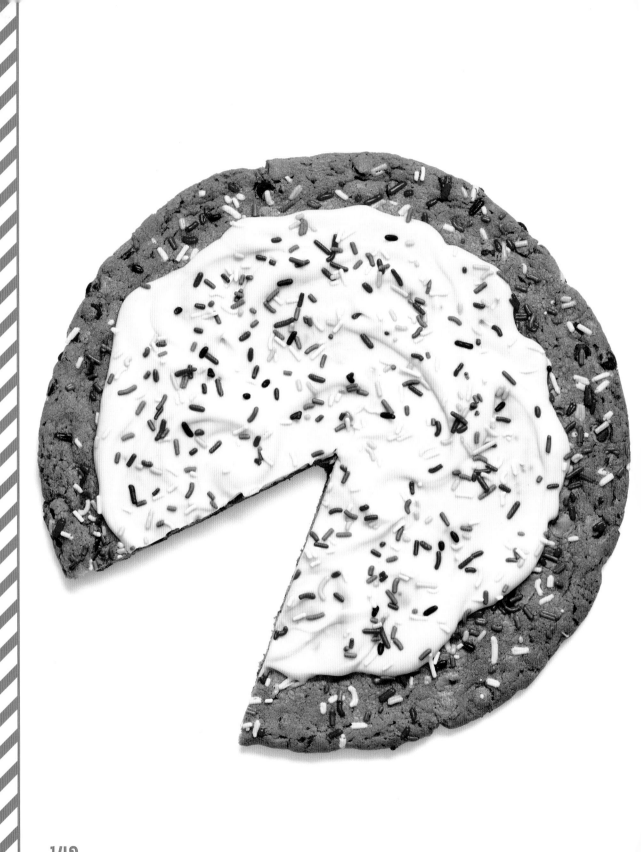

Confetti Cookie Pizza

ACTIVE: 10 min   TOTAL: 45 min   SERVES: 8 to 10

1   16-ounce tube
     refrigerated chocolate
     chip cookie dough

1   tablespoon rainbow
     sprinkles, plus more
     for topping

1   cup mascarpone cheese

¼   cup confectioners' sugar

½   teaspoon pure
     vanilla extract

1   Preheat the oven to 350˚. Line a baking sheet with parchment paper. Shape the cookie dough into a 9-inch round on the baking sheet. Top with the sprinkles.

2   Bake until lightly browned around the edges, 15 to 20 minutes; let cool completely on the baking sheet.

3   Combine the mascarpone, confectioners' sugar and vanilla in a medium bowl and whisk until smooth. Spread on the cooled cookie, leaving a small border. Top with more sprinkles. Slide the cookie pizza onto a cutting board and cut into wedges.

Tip
To make your cookie look like a real pizza, top with red frosting for the sauce and grated white chocolate for the cheese!

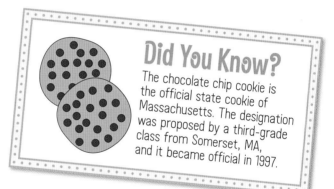

Did You Know?
The chocolate chip cookie is the official state cookie of Massachusetts. The designation was proposed by a third-grade class from Somerset, MA, and it became official in 1997.

Snack-Attack Chocolate Chip Cookies

ACTIVE: **25 min**   TOTAL: **50 min**   MAKES: **about 24**

- 1½ cups all-purpose flour
- ¾ teaspoon baking soda
- ½ teaspoon salt
- 1¼ sticks (10 tablespoons) unsalted butter, at room temperature
- 1 cup packed light brown sugar
- 1 large egg, at room temperature
- 1 teaspoon pure vanilla extract
- 1 cup semisweet chocolate chips or chunks
- 1 cup lightly crushed potato chips
- ½ cup broken pretzels

1 Preheat the oven to 375°. Combine the flour, baking soda and salt in a medium bowl and whisk to combine. Combine the butter and brown sugar in a large bowl and beat with a mixer on medium-high speed until pale and fluffy, 4 minutes. Add the egg and vanilla and beat until combined. Reduce the mixer speed to low and beat in the flour mixture until just combined. Stir in the chocolate chips, potato chips and pretzels with a rubber spatula.

2 Line 2 baking sheets with parchment paper. Roll the dough into 1½-inch balls with your hands and arrange the dough balls 2 inches apart on the baking sheets. Bake until set around the edges, 15 to 16 minutes. Let cool 10 minutes on the pans, then move the cookies to a rack with a spatula to cool completely.

Tip
Use a small ice cream scoop to portion your dough so you'll get evenly sized cookies.

Edible Cookie Dough

ACTIVE: **20 min**   TOTAL: **1 hr (plus 1 hr chilling)**   SERVES: **6**

1½ cups all-purpose flour

1½ sticks (12 tablespoons) unsalted butter, at room temperature

1 cup packed light brown sugar

1 teaspoon pure vanilla extract

½ teaspoon salt

¼ cup whole milk

1 cup semisweet chocolate chips

1 Preheat the oven to 350˚. Line a baking sheet with parchment paper, then spread the flour on the baking sheet. Bake until slightly darkened, 12 to 15 minutes. Gather the flour into a mound on the baking sheet and insert an instant-read thermometer into the center; it should register at least 160˚. If it doesn't, spread out the flour again and continue baking, rechecking the temperature every 3 to 5 minutes. Let cool completely, about 30 minutes.

2 Combine the butter, brown sugar, vanilla and salt in a large bowl and beat with a mixer on low speed until combined. Increase the mixer speed to medium high and continue to beat until pale and fluffy, about 3 minutes.

3 Reduce the mixer speed to low, add the toasted flour and beat until combined, about 30 seconds. Add the milk, increase the mixer speed to medium and beat until creamy, about 30 seconds. Stir in the chocolate chips with a rubber spatula. Refrigerate at least 1 hour or overnight.

Tip
Toasting the flour in step 1 is important— otherwise the dough is not safe to eat raw.

Did You Know?
One of Ben & Jerry's most popular ice cream flavors is Half Baked, which contains chunks of edible chocolate chip cookie dough and fudge brownies.

M&M Bar Cookies

ACTIVE: **25 min**   TOTAL: **1½ hr**   MAKES: **24**

Cooking spray

2 sticks unsalted butter,
   at room temperature

1 cup granulated sugar

1 cup packed
   light brown sugar

3 large eggs

1½ teaspoons pure
   vanilla extract

3 cups all-purpose flour

¾ teaspoon baking soda

¾ teaspoon salt

1½ cups M&M's

1 cup mini chocolate
   chips

1 Preheat the oven to 350°. Line a 9-by-13-inch baking dish with foil, leaving a 2-inch overhang on two sides; coat the foil with cooking spray.

2 Combine the butter, granulated sugar and brown sugar in a large bowl and beat with a mixer on medium-high speed until fluffy, about 4 minutes. Add the eggs and vanilla and beat until combined. Reduce the mixer speed to low. Add the flour, baking soda and salt and beat until combined. Stir in the M&M's and mini chocolate chips with a rubber spatula.

3 Scrape the dough into the prepared pan with the rubber spatula and press to the edges using damp or oiled fingers. Bake until a toothpick inserted into the center comes out clean, 35 to 40 minutes. Place the pan on a rack and let the bars cool completely in the pan.

4 Lift the bars out of the pan using the foil and move to a cutting board. Remove the foil and slice into pieces.

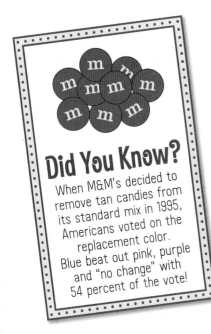

Did You Know?

When M&M's decided to remove tan candies from its standard mix in 1995, Americans voted on the replacement color. Blue beat out pink, purple and "no change" with 54 percent of the vote!

S'mores Cookie Dough Bars

ACTIVE: **15 min**   TOTAL: **2 hr**   MAKES: **24**

1 cup all-purpose flour
Cooking spray
1 stick unsalted butter, at room temperature
1 cup packed light brown sugar
1 teaspoon pure vanilla extract
2 cups finely ground graham crackers
1 14-ounce can condensed milk
1 cup milk chocolate chips
1 cup mini marshmallows

Tip
When you're making bar cookies and brownies, line the pan with foil, leaving some hanging over the edge. This will act as a handle so you can lift the finished bars out of the pan.

1 Preheat the oven to 350°. Line a baking sheet with parchment paper, then spread the flour on the baking sheet. Bake until slightly darkened, 12 to 15 minutes. Gather the flour into a mound on the baking sheet and insert an instant-read thermometer into the center; it should register at least 160°. If it doesn't, spread out the flour again and continue baking, rechecking the temperature every 3 to 5 minutes. Let cool completely, about 30 minutes.

2 Line a 9-by-13-inch baking dish with foil, leaving a 2-inch overhang on two sides; coat the foil with cooking spray.

3 Combine the butter, brown sugar and vanilla in a large bowl and beat with a mixer on medium-high speed until fluffy, about 4 minutes. Reduce the mixer speed to low. Add the graham cracker crumbs and toasted flour and beat until combined. Add the condensed milk and beat until combined. Stir in the chocolate chips and marshmallows with a rubber spatula.

4 Scrape the dough into the prepared pan with the rubber spatula and press to the edges using damp or oiled fingers. Refrigerate until set, at least 1 hour.

5 Lift the bars out of the pan using the foil and move to a cutting board. Remove the foil and slice into pieces.

DESIGN YOUR OWN RECIPE

Cereal Treats

❶ Choose Your Cereal
Use 7 cups total (pick 1 or 2 types).

Crispy rice cereal (regular or chocolate)   **Cornflakes**   **Corn or rice squares**   **Toasted oat cereal (regular or chocolate)**   **Graham cereal**   **Chocolate puffs**

❷ Make the Base
Line a 9-inch square baking dish with nonstick foil. Melt 6 tablespoons unsalted butter or coconut oil in a large pot over medium heat. Add one 10-ounce bag mini or regular marshmallows and stir with a wooden spoon until melted, then stir in 1 teaspoon vanilla. Stir in ½ cup nut butter, if you want. Remove from the heat and stir in the cereal.

❸ Add Mix-Ins
Stir in 1½ cups total (pick up to 3 types).

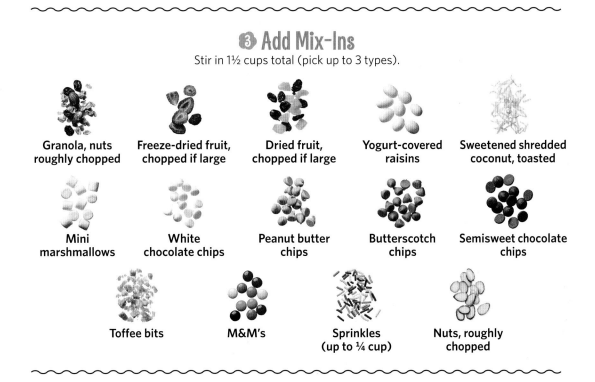

Granola, nuts roughly chopped   **Freeze-dried fruit, chopped if large**   **Dried fruit, chopped if large**   **Yogurt-covered raisins**   **Sweetened shredded coconut, toasted**

Mini marshmallows   **White chocolate chips**   **Peanut butter chips**   **Butterscotch chips**   **Semisweet chocolate chips**

Toffee bits   **M&M's**   **Sprinkles (up to ¼ cup)**   **Nuts, roughly chopped**

❹ Form the Bars
Press the cereal mixture into the prepared pan using a rubber spatula. Let cool, then lift out of the pan using the foil and move to a cutting board. Remove the foil and slice into pieces.

Brownie Pops

Cooking spray

2 cups semisweet chocolate chips

1 stick unsalted butter, cut into pieces

¾ cup granulated sugar

¾ cup packed light brown sugar

4 large eggs

1 teaspoon pure vanilla extract

1 cup all-purpose flour

½ teaspoon salt

1 cup chopped semisweet chocolate

4 teaspoons vegetable shortening

Chocolate sprinkles, for topping

1 Preheat the oven to 325°. Coat a 9-by-13-inch pan with cooking spray and line the pan with foil, leaving a 1-inch overhang on two sides. Coat the foil with more cooking spray.

2 Combine the chocolate chips and butter in a saucepan over low heat and cook, whisking, until melted. Remove the pan from the heat and whisk in the granulated sugar and brown sugar; let cool slightly.

3 Whisk the eggs into the chocolate mixture, one at a time, then whisk in the vanilla. Stir in the flour and salt with a wooden spoon.

4 Scrape the batter into the prepared pan and spread evenly. Bake until set, about 45 minutes. Place the pan on a rack and let the brownies cool completely in the pan.

5 Lift the brownies out of the pan using the foil and move to a cutting board. Remove the foil and slice into small squares; insert a lollipop stick into each.

6 Line a baking sheet with parchment paper. Microwave the chopped chocolate with the shortening in a small microwave-safe bowl, stirring every 30 seconds, until melted. Dip the brownies in the melted chocolate and place on the baking sheet. Top with chocolate sprinkles and let set.

Did You Know?

Chocolate grows on trees—sort of! It's made from cocoa beans, which come from the cacao tree.

Caramel Corn Milkshakes

ACTIVE: 10 min   TOTAL: 10 min   MAKES: 2 to 4

1 cup caramel corn,
plus more for topping

1 pint vanilla ice cream,
slightly softened

½ cup milk

Pinch of salt

Caramel sauce, for drizzling

1 Pulse the caramel corn in a blender until finely ground.
Add the ice cream, milk and salt and blend until smooth.

2 Pour the milkshake into glasses, top with more caramel
corn and drizzle with caramel sauce.

Tip
If you have extra caramel corn, try mixing it with cheddar popcorn. It's a popular combo in Chicago—and it's surprisingly delicious!

Did You Know?
The blender was invented in 1922 for making milkshakes. Before that time, most milkshakes were mixed by hand. Sounds like a workout!

Chocolate Chip Cookie Pudding

ACTIVE: **20 min**   TOTAL: **25 min (plus 2 hour chilling)**   SERVES: **4**

½ **cup sugar**

2 **tablespoons cornstarch**

⅛ **teaspoon salt**

2 **cups whole milk**

1 **large egg**

1 **tablespoon pure vanilla extract**

1 **tablespoon unsalted butter**

½ **cup milk chocolate chips**

4 **chocolate chip cookies, crumbled**

1 Combine the sugar, cornstarch and salt in a medium bowl; slowly whisk in 1 cup milk until smooth, then whisk in the egg.

2 Bring the remaining 1 cup milk to a boil in a medium saucepan over medium heat. Remove from the heat and whisk in the sugar mixture. Cook over medium-low heat, whisking, until thick and creamy, 5 to 7 minutes. Remove from the heat again and whisk in the vanilla and butter until smooth. Whisk in the chocolate chips.

3 Spoon the pudding into 4 ramekins or small dishes, layering it with some of the crumbled cookies. Press plastic wrap onto the surface and refrigerate until set, about 2 hours. Top with the remaining crumbled cookies.

Tip
Press a piece of plastic wrap directly onto the surface of your pudding before you put it in the fridge. This will prevent a skin from forming.

What's Your Ice Cream Truck IQ?

Take this quiz, then listen for your neighborhood truck!

1 **Which of these popular chains started as an ice cream truck?**

BR baskin robbins®

A. Baskin-Robbins

DQ®

B. Dairy Queen

Carvel®

C. Carvel

COLD STONE CREAMERY®

D. Cold Stone Creamery

2 **Circle the three flavors in a Popsicle-brand snow cone.**

Strawberry	Sour Apple
Orange	**Grape**
Lemon	**Blue Raspberry**

3 **What's the most popular Popsicle flavor in the US?**

A. Grape

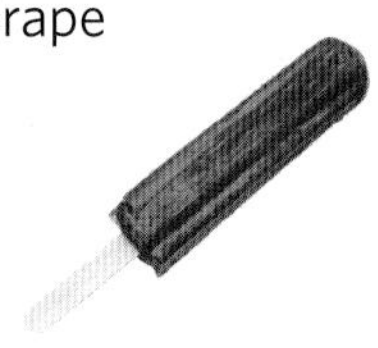

B. Cherry

C. Orange

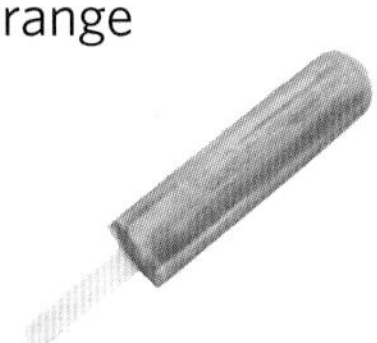

D. Blue Raspberry

4 Can you ID these frozen treats?

_____ **1.** Chocolate Éclair   _____ **4.** Fudgsicle   _____ **7.** Pop Up

_____ **2.** Strawberry Shortcake   _____ **5.** Scribbler   _____ **8.** Klondike Bar

_____ **3.** Creamsicle   _____ **6.** Firecracker   _____ **9.** FatBoy

5 Which of these cartoon characters has been turned into a frozen treat?

A. Tweety Bird

B. SpongeBob SquarePants

C. Hello Kitty

D. Spider-Man

E. All of the above

6 How did the Good Humor company get its name?

A. The founder was a comedian on the side.

B. When the company was founded, ice cream was thought to improve a person's mood.

C. The founder's last name was Humor.

D. The company was founded on April Fools' Day.

Answers: 1 C; **2** Strawberry, lemon and blue raspberry; **3** B; **4** F; **2** B; **3** D; **4** H; **5** I; **6** A; **7** C; **8** G; **9** E; **5** E; **6** B

Fake-Out Cakes

Cheeseburger Cake

ACTIVE: **45 min**   TOTAL: **2 hr**   SERVES: **14 to 16**

Cooking spray

2   15- to 16-ounce boxes
     chocolate cake mix

8   large eggs

2   cups buttermilk

1   cup vegetable oil

¼   cup green sanding sugar

8   spearmint leaf gummy candies

Cornstarch, for dusting

3   ounces orange fondant

1   16-ounce tub vanilla frosting

1   16-ounce tub chocolate frosting

¾   teaspoon yellow food coloring

5   drops red food coloring

2   tablespoons crispy rice cereal

Tip
Fondant, which we used to make the fake cheese, is like Play-Doh—it can dry out easily. Wrap leftover pieces tightly in plastic wrap so you can use them again.

1 Preheat the oven to 350°. Coat a 2½-quart ovenproof bowl and two 8-inch round cake pans with cooking spray. Combine the cake mix, eggs, buttermilk and vegetable oil in a large bowl and beat with a mixer until smooth.

2 Pour the batter into the ovenproof bowl and pans; bake until a toothpick inserted into the centers comes out clean, about 25 minutes for the pans and about 45 minutes for the bowl. Let cool in the pans 15 minutes, then remove the cakes to racks to cool completely.

3 Make the lettuce: Sprinkle some green sanding sugar on a cutting board. Roll out the spearmint candies to about ⅛ inch thick with a rolling pin, sprinkling with more sugar to keep the candies from sticking.

4 Cut each flattened gummy piece into 3 strips with a paring knife. Fold each strip like an accordion to make ruffles; pinch the ends together with your fingers.

5 Make the cheese: Dust a cutting board with cornstarch. Roll out the orange fondant to about ⅛ inch thick with the rolling pin. Trim the fondant into a 7-inch square with the paring knife; cover with plastic wrap and set aside.

6 Make the buns: Trim the top of 1 round cake and the flat side of the bowl cake with a serrated knife; set the trimmings aside. Mix the vanilla frosting, ¼ cup chocolate frosting and the food coloring to make a light brown frosting.

7 Assemble the bottom bun: Put the trimmed round cake on a cardboard round or serving plate. Spread some of the light brown frosting over the cake with an offset spatula. Arrange the candy lettuce around the edge.

8 Make the patty: Spread the remaining chocolate frosting over the top and sides of the untrimmed round cake. Crumble the cake trimmings and press them into the frosting.

9 Put the chocolate patty on the bottom bun, then drape the orange fondant cheese on top. Cover the bowl-shaped cake with the remaining light brown frosting; place on the patty. Press the rice cereal into the frosting.

Strawberry Crunch Ice Cream Cake

ACTIVE: **45 min**   TOTAL: **2 hr (plus 1 hr freezing)**   SERVES: **12 to 16**

- 1 **15- to 16-ounce box vanilla cake mix (plus required ingredients)**
- 1 **1½-quart rectangular carton strawberry ice cream**
- 1 **1.2-ounce bag freeze-dried strawberries, crumbled (1½ cups)**
- 1 **16-ounce tub white frosting**

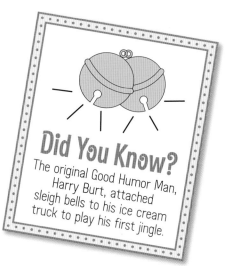

Did You Know?
The original Good Humor Man, Harry Burt, attached sleigh bells to his ice cream truck to play his first jingle.

Tip
Be sure to use a rectangular carton of ice cream for this recipe. You can slice it while it's frozen—which is a lot easier (and less messy!) than scooping.

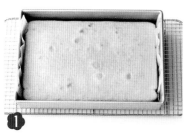

1 Preheat the oven to 350°. Line a 9-by-13-inch pan with parchment paper, leaving an overhang. Prepare the cake mix as the label directs. Spread the batter in the pan. Bake and cool as the label directs.

2 Trim the domed top of the cake with a serrated knife to make it level. Cut the cake in half horizontally to make 2 thin layers. Trim ¾-inch strips from each long side; reserve the strips and trimmings.

3 Cut the carton off the ice cream with kitchen scissors and set the ice cream block on a cutting board. Slice lengthwise into thirds with a large knife.

4 Put the ice cream on the bottom layer of the cake. Let soften slightly, then smooth with an offset spatula to cover the cake, leaving a ¾-inch border on the long sides.

5 Press 1 reserved strip of cake against each long side of the ice cream layer. Reserve the remaining 2 strips of cake. Place the second cake layer on top of the ice cream. Carefully slide onto a baking sheet and freeze 1 hour.

6 Remove the cake from the freezer. Cut off a corner of the frozen cake to look like a bite. Remove the ice cream from the trimmed bite and reserve the cake trimmings. Return the cake to the freezer.

7 Preheat the oven to 350°. Crumble the reserved cake strips and trimmings on a baking sheet. Bake, carefully tossing occasionally, until golden, 10 minutes. Let cool, then crumble the cake along with the dried strawberries.

8 Finely crush 1 tablespoon of the strawberry-crumb mixture; mix with 1 tablespoon frosting to make it pink. Spread the remaining white frosting over the cake with an offset spatula. Press the strawberry-crumb mixture into the frosting (do not cover the bite).

9 Spread the pink frosting inside the bite in a line. Add a line of the strawberry-crumb mixture at the bottom of the bite. Freeze until firm, at least 15 minutes. Insert a wooden spatula handle or large craft stick into the end of the cake opposite the bite before serving.

Giant S'more Cake

ACTIVE: **45 min**   TOTAL: **1 hr 40 min (plus 1 hr freezing)**
SERVES: **12 to 14**

1   **17.5-ounce bag sugar cookie mix**
    (plus required ingredients)

¾   **cup finely ground graham crackers**
    (about 7)

1   **11-ounce jar hot fudge topping**

1   **1.5-quart rectangular carton**
    vanilla ice cream

6   **large egg whites**

Pinch of cream of tartar

1   **cup sugar**

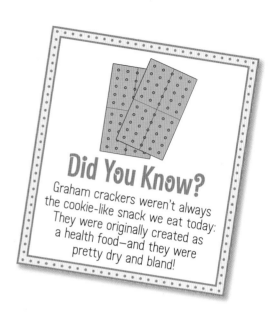

Did You Know?

Graham crackers weren't always the cookie-like snack we eat today: They were originally created as a health food—and they were pretty dry and bland!

Tip

Ask a grown-up to toast the meringue. Kitchen torches can be dangerous if you haven't had a lot of practice.

1

Make the large graham crackers: Preheat the oven to 350° and scoop out ¾ cup of the cookie mix (you won't need it). Prepare the remaining mix as the label directs for cut-outs, adding the ground graham crackers.

2

Divide the dough in half. Roll out each piece of dough with a rolling pin into a 9½-inch square on 2 separate sheets of parchment paper; transfer the dough and parchment to 2 baking sheets.

3

Bake the graham-cracker cookies until golden and set, 12 to 15 minutes. While still warm, carefully trim the edges with a paring knife to make even 9-inch squares.

4

Use a butter knife to score a dotted line across the middle of each cookie, then use a chopstick or skewer to make small holes as shown. Let cool completely on the baking sheets.

5

Using an offset spatula, spread the fudge sauce into a wavy pool on 1 cookie. Place in the freezer.

6

Let the ice cream soften slightly, then cut the carton off with kitchen scissors and set the ice cream block on its side on a piece of plastic wrap. Cover with more plastic and press to flatten slightly. Freeze until firm, about 1 hour.

7

Meanwhile, make the meringue: Combine the egg whites and cream of tartar in a large bowl and beat with a mixer on medium-high speed until foamy, then slowly beat in the sugar on high speed until stiff glossy peaks form.

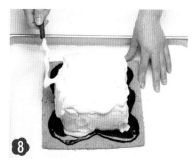

8

Make the marshmallow center: Remove the ice cream from the freezer and remove the plastic; set the ice cream on top of the fudge-covered cookie. Using the offset spatula, cover the ice cream with a thick layer of meringue.

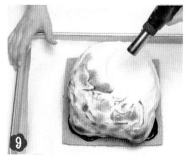

9

Ask a grown-up to use a kitchen torch to brown the meringue, then gently press the other graham cracker cookie on top. Freeze until ready to serve. Let soften slightly before slicing.

Candy Bar Cake

ACTIVE: **45 min**   TOTAL: **1 hr (plus 1 hr freezing)**
SERVES: **10 to 12**

FOR THE CAKE

- 1   12-ounce frozen pound cake
- 3   ounces semisweet chocolate, finely chopped
- 1½   sticks (12 tablespoons) unsalted butter, at room temperature
- 3 to 4 tablespoons milk
- 1   1-pound box confectioners' sugar
- ¾   cup salted roasted peanuts
- 2   cups dulce de leche

FOR THE COATING

- 10   ounces semisweet chocolate, finely chopped
- 1   stick cold unsalted butter, cut into pieces

Did You Know?

The Snickers bar was named after a horse! The animal was a favorite of the Mars family, creators of the candy.

Tip

Get your pound cake from the freezer aisle for this recipe: Frozen cakes are denser and easier to carve than the ones from the bakery department.

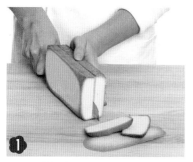

Assemble the cake: Trim ½ inch off the short ends of the pound cake with a serrated knife, then trim the domed top to make it flat. Stand the cake on its side and slice in half horizontally to make two equal-size rectangles.

Microwave the chocolate in a microwave-safe bowl, stirring every 30 seconds, until melted. Beat the butter, 3 tablespoons milk and the confectioners' sugar in a large bowl with a mixer. Beat in the melted chocolate. Add more milk, if needed, to make the frosting spreadable.

Lay the cake rectangles on a rack set on a rimmed baking sheet. Spread some of the frosting on one short end of each cake and press together to form a long rectangle. (You can slide a thin piece of cardboard under the cake for moving to a platter later.)

Spread the remaining frosting on the cake in a 1-inch-thick layer, making the edges slightly higher than the center. Smooth the top and sides with an offset spatula. Freeze until firm, about 30 minutes.

Combine the peanuts and dulce de leche in a bowl and stir to combine.

Remove the cake from the freezer. Spread the peanut mixture over the frosting in a flat, even layer with a spoon. Freeze until the peanut mixture is firm, about 30 minutes.

Meanwhile, make the chocolate coating: Microwave the chocolate and butter in a microwave-safe bowl, stirring every 30 seconds, until melted and smooth. Scrape into a liquid measuring cup.

Pour the chocolate coating on the cake and spread it evenly over the top and sides with an offset spatula. Freeze until the chocolate cools slightly, 6 to 8 minutes.

Remove the cake from the freezer. Dip the edge of the offset spatula into the chocolate at an angle, starting at a short end, and gently pull up, repeating along the cake to create a wave pattern. Refrigerate 10 minutes before slicing.

PB&J Sandwich Cake

ACTIVE: **25 min**   TOTAL: **1½ hr**   SERVES: **8 to 10**

1   stick unsalted butter, at room temperature, plus more for the pan

All-purpose flour, for the pan

1   15- to 16-ounce box white cake mix (plus required ingredients)

1   cup creamy peanut butter

1½ to 2 cups confectioners' sugar

2 to 3 tablespoons milk

¾   cup grape jelly

Did You Know?
More than 500 peanuts go into a single 12-ounce jar of peanut butter!

Tip
When you're making frosting with confectioners' sugar, add the sugar gradually on low speed. Otherwise it will fly all over the place!

1 Preheat the oven to 350°. Butter a 9-inch-square cake pan, line with parchment, then butter again and dust with flour. Prepare the cake mix as the label directs and fill the pan three-quarters full (you may have batter left over). Bake until a toothpick inserted into the center comes out clean, 30 to 35 minutes.

2 Let the cake cool in the pan 10 minutes, then carefully remove to a rack and let cool completely. Place the cake on a cutting board. Trim the domed top of the cake with a serrated knife to make it level. Cut the cake in half horizontally to make 2 thin layers.

3 Combine the butter and peanut butter in a large bowl and beat with a mixer until smooth. Slowly add the confectioners' sugar, alternating with the milk and beating after each addition, until the frosting is fluffy and smooth. In a small bowl, whisk the grape jelly until it is loose and spreadable.

4 Spread a thick layer of peanut butter frosting on the bottom cake half with an offset spatula.

5 Spread the grape jelly on top of the peanut butter frosting with the offset spatula, making sure to reach the edges. Top with the remaining cake layer.

6 Cut the cake in half diagonally with a chef's knife and place on a serving plate. Separate the halves slightly to show the filling.

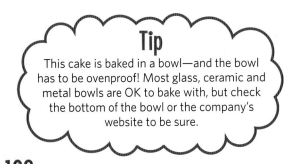

Cereal Bowl Cake

ACTIVE: **45 min**   TOTAL: **2½ hr (plus 2½ hr freezing)**   SERVES: **8 to 10**

Cooking spray

1   **15- to 16-ounce box chocolate cake mix (plus required ingredients)**

1   **16-ounce tub vanilla frosting**

1   **pint vanilla ice cream**

1   **cup Froot Loops or other cereal**

Tip

This cake is baked in a bowl—and the bowl has to be ovenproof! Most glass, ceramic and metal bowls are OK to bake with, but check the bottom of the bowl or the company's website to be sure.

Did You Know?

When Froot Loops were introduced in 1963, they came in only three colors: red, orange and yellow. The other colors (green, purple and blue) were added almost 30 years later!

1

Preheat the oven to 350°. Coat a 2½-quart ovenproof bowl with cooking spray. Prepare the cake mix as the label directs; pour into the bowl. Bake until a toothpick inserted into the center comes out clean, about 1 hour. Let cool completely.

2

Remove the cake from the bowl. Trim the flat side of the cake with a long serrated knife to make it level.

3

Use a small serrated knife to cut a circle into the top of the cake, about ¾ inch in from the edge and 1½ inches deep. Use your fingers or a fork to pull out the cake in the middle.

4

Flip the cake over onto a cardboard circle or wax paper–lined plate. Spread the frosting over the cake with an offset spatula, leaving the flat part unfrosted at the top.

5

Cut out a small cardboard circle and place on the unfrosted area. Flip the cake over onto another piece of wax paper.

6

Spread more frosting over the lip and the inside of the cake (the inside doesn't have to be perfect—it will be covered with ice cream). Freeze until the frosting sets, 30 minutes.

7

Dip the offset spatula in hot water and wipe dry; use it to smooth out the frosting.

8

Microwave the ice cream in a microwave-safe bowl on 50-percent power until softened but not melted, about 30 seconds. Spoon into the cake and smooth with the spatula.

9

Sprinkle the cereal on top and gently press into the ice cream. Freeze until firm, at least 2 hours. Add a spoon before serving.

Fried Chicken Cake Pops

ACTIVE: **1 hr**   TOTAL: **2½ hr**   MAKES: **16**

Cooking spray
1   **15- to 16-ounce box chocolate cake mix (plus required ingredients)**
1   **cup cream cheese frosting**
16 **mini marshmallows**
16 **pretzel sticks**
2   **cups white candy melts**
1   **12-ounce package butterscotch chips**
2 to 4 tablespoons coconut oil
¼   **cup crushed cornflakes**
Flaky sea salt, for topping

Did You Know?

The original handwritten recipe for KFC's fried chicken breading is locked in a vault at the company's headquarters in Kentucky.

Tip

You can use this recipe to make regular cake pops. Just form the crumbled cake mixture into balls and insert lollipop sticks, freeze until firm, then dip in melted candy melts.

①

Preheat the oven to 350°. Coat a 9-by-13-inch cake pan with cooking spray. Prepare the cake mix as the label directs. Spread the batter in the pan with a rubber spatula. Bake and cool as the label directs.

②

Crumble the cake in a large bowl. Add the frosting and mix with your hands until fully combined.

③

Using damp hands, form the mixture into 16 compact egg shapes (2 to 2½ inches long), pinching each slightly in the center. Arrange on 2 parchment-lined baking sheets.

④

Stick a mini marshmallow on one end of each pretzel, then insert into the cake balls, reshaping as needed. Return the drumsticks to the baking sheets. Freeze until slightly firm, 15 to 20 minutes.

⑤

Microwave the candy melts in a small microwave-safe bowl, stirring every 30 seconds, until melted. Dip the marshmallow-topped pretzels in the candy melts; return to the baking sheets and refrigerate until set. Redip to form a thicker coating; refrigerate.

⑥

Microwave the butterscotch chips with 2 tablespoons coconut oil in a separate microwave-safe bowl, stirring every 30 seconds, until melted (add more coconut oil as needed until pourable). Stir in the cereal. Spoon the mixture over the cake part to coat; sprinkle with salt. Return to the baking sheet and refrigerate until set.

Ice Cream Steak and Fries

ACTIVE: **30 min**   TOTAL: **1 hr 10 min (plus 1½ hr freezing)**
MAKES: **4 plates (serves 8)**

FOR THE STEAKS

1   1½-quart cylindrical carton chocolate ice cream
½   cup finely crushed chocolate wafer cookies

FOR THE FRIES

2   12-ounce frozen pound cakes, thawed
1   stick unsalted butter, melted
½   cup seedless strawberry jam

Did You Know?
Americans like french fries, but Belgians like them even more: They eat more fries per person than any other country in the world!

1 Make the steaks: Using a serrated knife, slice the ice cream carton crosswise into 4 rounds, dipping the knife in hot water as needed. Cut the carton off with kitchen scissors.

2 Tightly wrap each ice cream round in plastic wrap, then form into a steak shape with your hands (the warmth of your hands will soften the ice cream). Freeze until firm, about 30 minutes.

3 Unwrap one ice cream steak and place on a piece of parchment or wax paper. Run a metal skewer under hot water, then press into the ice cream to create parallel diagonal grill-mark lines.

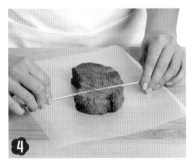

4 Make lines in the opposite direction to form a crosshatch pattern, running the skewer under hot water as needed. If the ice cream gets too soft, return to the freezer until firm.

5 Sprinkle the chocolate wafer crumbs into the lines. Slide the ice cream steak onto a baking sheet and freeze until firm, about 30 minutes. Repeat with the remaining steaks.

6 Make the fries: Using a crinkle vegetable cutter or a chef's knife, trim the sides of the pound cakes, then cut each cake crosswise into ¼-inch thick slices.

7 Cut each pound cake slice into sticks. Divide between 2 parchment-lined rimmed baking sheets. Preheat the oven to 350°.

8 Drizzle the melted butter over the cake fries and toss. Bake, carefully tossing the fries halfway through, until lightly toasted, about 8 minutes; let cool slightly.

9 Arrange the cake steaks and fries on plates and serve with small bowls of strawberry jam.

Sicilian Pizza Cake

ACTIVE: **45 min**   TOTAL: **1½ hr**   SERVES: **10 to 12**

Cooking spray
2   **15- to 16-ounce boxes white cake mix**
     (plus required ingredients)
5 to 6 strips all-natural
     berry-flavored fruit leather
8   **ounces white chocolate**
1   **16- to 18-ounce jar strawberry preserves**
     (not jelly)

Did You Know?
The biggest day for
pizza-eating in the US
is Super Bowl Sunday.
Halloween is a close second.
The least amount of pizza is
consumed on Thanksgiving.

1 Preheat the oven to 350°. Coat the bottom and sides of an 11-by-17-inch rimmed baking sheet with cooking spray. Prepare the cake mixes as the label directs. Spread the batter in the pan with a rubber spatula, filling it three-quarters full (you'll have batter left over).

2 Bake the cake until a toothpick inserted into the center comes out clean, 15 to 20 minutes. Let cool completely in the pan, then scrape off the top of the cake with a fork, leaving a border for the crust.

3 Cut the fruit leather into 1½-inch circles using a cookie cutter or kitchen scissors and set aside. (If the strips are too narrow, roll them out slightly with a rolling pin before cutting.)

4 Grate about 2 tablespoons of the white chocolate into a bowl with a fine grater; set aside. Chop the remaining white chocolate with a chef's knife.

5 Microwave the chopped white chocolate in a microwave-safe bowl, stirring every 30 seconds, until melted and smooth.

6 Mix the strawberry preserves with 2 tablespoons of the melted white chocolate in another bowl—this will make it look more like pizza sauce.

7 Spread the strawberry mixture on the cake inside the border using a spoon.

8 Top with spoonfuls of the melted white chocolate, spreading each slightly with the back of the spoon to look like melted cheese. Sprinkle with the grated white chocolate.

9 Ask a grown-up to brown the melted white chocolate and the edges of the cake with a kitchen torch. Top with the fruit-leather circles.

Mac and Cheese Cake

ACTIVE: **40 min**   TOTAL: **3 hr**   SERVES: **8 to 10**

Cooking spray
1   15- to 16-ounce box yellow cake mix
      (plus required ingredients)
1   cup orange candy melts
1   cup yellow candy melts
2   16-ounce tubs white frosting
Orange and yellow gel food coloring

1 Preheat the oven to 325°. Coat a 2½-quart ovenproof bowl with cooking spray. Prepare the cake mix as the label directs; pour into the bowl.

2 Bake the cake in the bowl until a toothpick inserted into the center comes out clean, 50 minutes to 1 hour. Let cool slightly, then remove from the bowl to a rack to cool completely.

3 Meanwhile, make the macaroni: Combine the orange and yellow candy melts in a large microwave-safe bowl and microwave, stirring every 30 seconds, until melted. Let cool slightly.

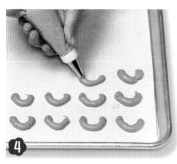

4 Spoon the melted candy into a piping bag fitted with a ¼-inch round tip. Pipe 50 to 60 elbows onto a parchment-lined baking sheet. Let set, about 20 minutes.

5 Put the bowl cake flat-side up. Use a small paring knife to score a rim around the top of the cake, about ½ inch in from the edge. Carve out a little of the cake inside the rim with the knife to create a bowl.

6 Flip the bowl cake upside down onto a separate parchment-lined baking sheet and spread the frosting over the sides with an offset spatula, leaving the middle bare. (You'll flip it and this will become the bottom.) Freeze until firm, about 1 hour.

7 Flip the bowl cake right-side up. Spread more frosting over the rim with the offset spatula, reserving about ¾ cup frosting.

8 Tint the reserved frosting orange using orange and yellow food coloring. Spoon the frosting into a piping bag fitted with the same ¼-inch round tip. Pipe squiggles of orange frosting inside the rim of the cake.

9 Remove the candy macaroni from the baking sheet and arrange on top of the cake.

POP QUIZ

Do You Know Your Candy?

See if you can match these candy names to the pictures.

A. Jolly Ranchers   **D.** Dots   **G.** SweeTarts   **J.** Runts

B. Tootsie Rolls   **E.** Twizzlers Nibs   **H.** Atomic Fireballs   **K.** Smarties

C. Skittles   **F.** Nerds   **I.** Lemonheads   **L.** Now & Laters

1. _____

2. _____

3. _____

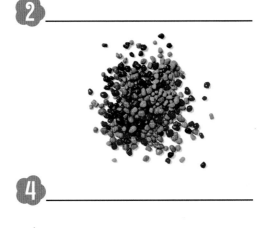

4. _____

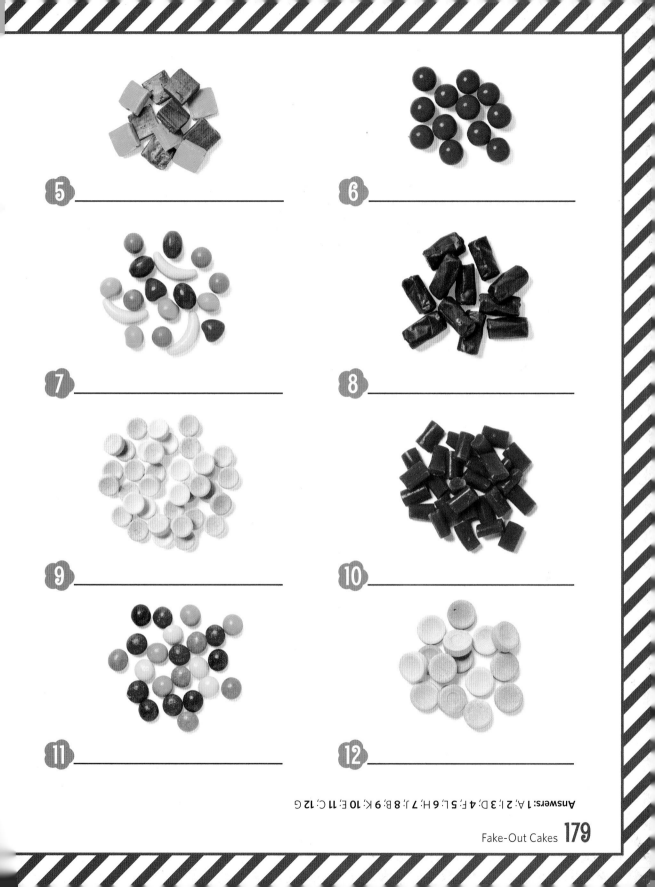

5 _____

6 _____

7 _____

8 _____

9 _____

10 _____

11 _____

12 _____

Color an ear of corn on page 186!

Coloring Book

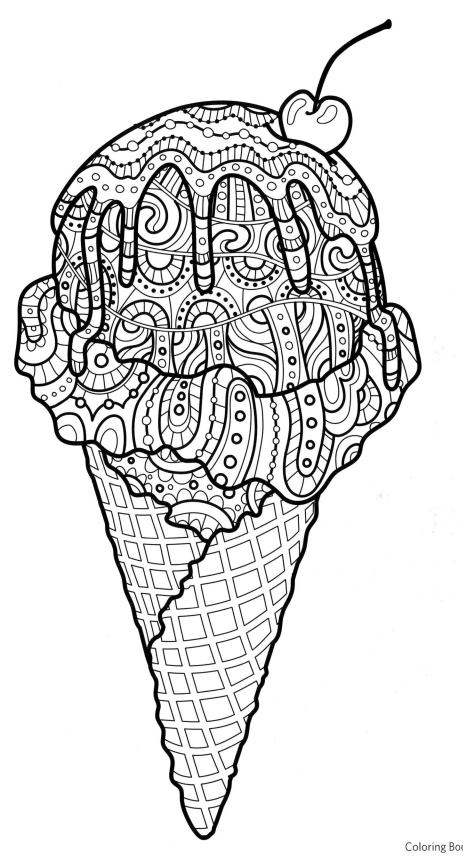

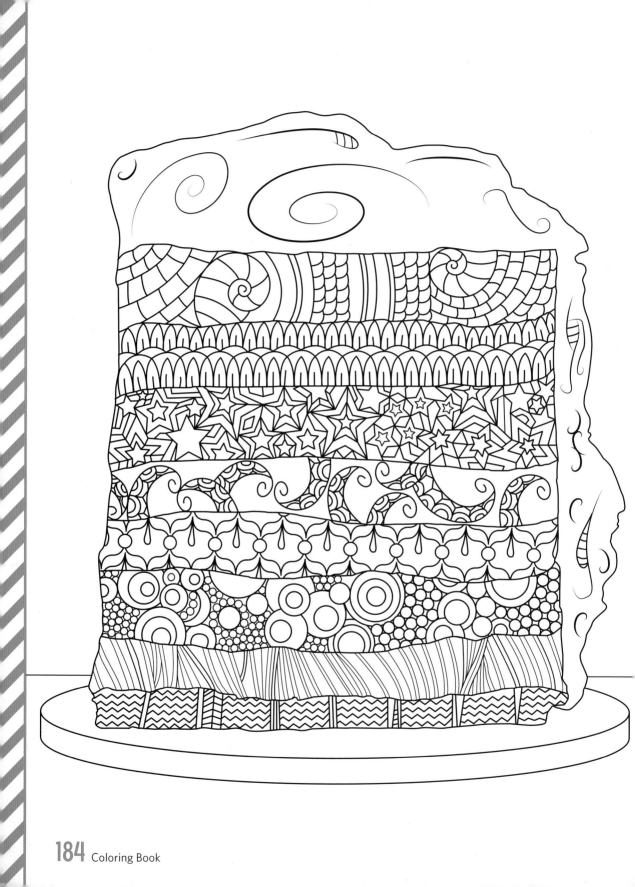

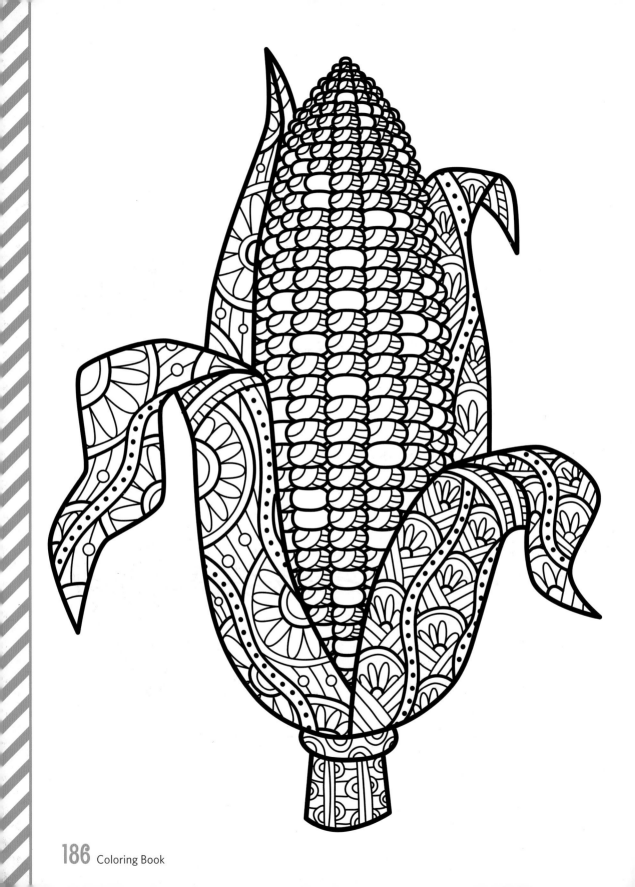

INDEX

INDEX